BULLYPROOF YOUR CHILD

BULLYPROOF YOUR CHILD

Keith Vitali
with Adam Brouillard

SKYHORSE PUBLISHING

www.skyhorsepublishing.com

10 9 8 7 6 5 4 3 2 1

Library of Congress Cataloging-in-Publication Data

Vitali, Keith.
Bullyproof your child : expert advice on teaching children to defend themselves / Keith Vitali with Adam Brouillard.
      p. cm. — (Bullyproof your child)
  Includes index.
  ISBN 978-1-60239-076-8 (alk. paper)
  1. Bullying. 2. Child rearing. I. Brouillard, Adam. II. Title.

BF637.B85V58 2007
303.6'9—dc22

                              2007024998

Printed in the United States of America

CONTENTS

Foreword by Dr. Jose Luis Hinojosa   vii

Introduction   ix

Chapter 1: What is Bullying?   1
    Keith Vitali's Bullying Story   1
    Bullying Behavior   2
    Gender Differences in Bullying   3

Chapter 2: Bullying Statistics   5
    Other Statistics   6
    Long-Term Effects of Bullying   6
    Bullying and Gangs   7

Chapter 3: When Should a Child Fight Back?   9
    Myth Versus Fact   10
    A Self-Defense Course for Your Child   11
    Bullying Scenarios   11

Chapter 4: The Increase in Bullying in America   13
    My Perspective   13
    The Solution   17
    Who Are the Bullies?   18
    Keith Vitali's Four Action Steps to Decrease Bullying in America   18

Chapter 5: How Bullies Choose their Victims   21
    Choosing Victims Subconsciously   22
    Shopping-for-a-Shirt Theory   23
    Racially Motivated Bullying   23

Chapter 6: If Your Child is Being Bullied   25
    What You Can Do   26
    Talking to a Teacher or Principal   27
    Asking an Older Child to Talk to the Bully   27
    Steps to Take If Your Child is Being Bullied   28

Chapter 7: If Your Child is the Bully   31
    Common Characteristics of Bullies   31
    Athletes Who Bully   32
    Verbal Bullies   32
    Cyberbullies   32

What Can Parents Do?   33
Solution   34

Chapter 8: The Martial Arts Edge   **35**
Transforming One Delinquent   36
Transforming All the Delinquents   37
Using Positive Reinforcement   37
Parent's One-Time Rule and Personal Responsibility Rule   38
Bullying Stories   41
Helping Your Child Gain Confidence   44

Chapter 9: Verbal Strategies for Dealing with a Bully   **45**
Scenario 1—Mockery   46
Scenario 2—Spreading Rumors   46
Scenario 3—Lunchtime Bully   47
Scenario 4—Playground Bully   48
Scenario 5—Physically Threatening Bully   48

Chapter 10: Standing Up to the Bully   **51**
Fighting Versus Self-Defense   51
Awareness and Avoidance   52
Walk Away   52
Taking an Assertive Stand   53
Defending Yourself Physically   53

Chapter 11: The Physical Confrontation   **55**
Confident Stances   55
Defensive Blocking Techniques   58
Self-Defense Techniques   80
Offensive Moves   100
Defense against a Frontal Choke   100
Defense against a Headlock   107
Defense against a Rear Bear Hug   112
Defense against a One-Armed Attack from the Rear   114

Chapter 12: Ground Defenses   **117**
The Elbows-and-Arms Block   118
Escaping from the Mount Position   119
Controlling the Bully on the Ground   121

Sources and Resources   **123**

Acknowledgments   **125**

About the Author   **127**

Bullyproof Journal   **129**

FOREWORD

For many children, starting school can be a frightening experience. School-age children will face a series of challenges, often for the first time in their lives, and their parents will probably not be there to help.

The medical community firmly believes that bullying deserves serious attention and preventive intervention, in order to help alleviate this epidemic that is endangering school-aged children all over America. And this is exactly what my good friend Keith Vitali, world-renowned children's self-defense expert and world champion martial artist, addresses in *Bullyproof Your Child*. He tackles school challenges in true championship fashion. Keith describes, in an easy-to-read approach, possible solutions to many of the problems associated with the everyday bully. He covers this important problem in a comprehensive fashion, and I'm proud of him for doing that. And because of the timeliness and significance of the subject matter, I would encourage parents to sit down and read this book with their children. Besides being a great bonding opportunity, it will also be a great learning experience for everyone. I am confident the information found in *Bullyproof Your Child* will teach you and your child some valuable lessons—not only for school but also for life.

—*Jose Luis Hinojosa, MD*
Medical Director, Hollywood Medical Center
www.GrandChampionGame.com

INTRODUCTION

Bullyproof Your Child should be the book all parents will choose if their child is having trouble with a bully. First of all, and most importantly, I'm a proud father of two grown children, Jennifer and Travis. I'm also a product of a large Italian family; the second-oldest of eight kids—four boys and four girls. This alone qualifies me as a children's expert on many levels, as other parents can attest.

As a child, I myself had many experiences with bullying. Not only was I bullied by other children but I was also the bully at times, mainly targeting my younger brothers. The fact is that most of us have been the bully at one time or another, so I'm not quick to condemn all bullies outright. Sometimes they know not what they do.

I'm also a black belt in karate, with over thirty-five years of experience teaching martial arts. During my time as an instructor, parents, doctors, teachers, principals, school counselors, child psychiatrists, and a host of other professionals have referred their children to my martial arts school to deal with their bullying issues. The sad truth about bullying is that almost every child has his own story of being bullied; it's that overwhelming and consuming of a problem in our society.

In this instructional manual for parents, I'm going to share with you some lessons I've learned from my students, and insights from my martial arts background, that have enabled my students and I to be tremendously successful when dealing with the everyday bully.

In this book, I'll offer strategies to deals with bullies on all levels, hopefully defusing any threatening situation before a confrontation can occur. In the event that there is an altercation, however, I will also offer safe and effective self-defensive strategies to help keep your child out of harm's way.

The following topics are covered in this book.

- How to avoid the everyday bully
- How to walk away from name-calling
- How to talk his way out of confrontation
- What to do if he's verbally bullied on a continuing basis
- Where to go if he feels physically threatened
- When he should stand up to a bully
- How to stand up to the bully
- Teaching him basic self defense skills.

There is an entirely different method of martial arts training, not covered in this book, that I call Stranger Danger. Stranger Danger refers to situations that are life-threatening, demanding an entirely different approach to self-defense, where the primary goal for the child is to inflict as much pain on his assailant as possible as he strives to get away from the attacker. I recommend that you enroll your child in a local martial arts school for this type of instruction.

Here is a universal truth about bullying—nine times out of ten, a child is picked on by someone he knows: someone at school, a playmate at the park, or a brother or sister at home. That's why this book will show you how to teach your children how to handle bullies in a safe, effective manner that doesn't hurt the other child.

BULLYPROOF YOUR CHILD

1
What is Bullying?

KEITH VITALI'S BULLYING STORY

I was eight years old when I encountered my first bullying incident. My dad had driven me to baseball tryouts at a local ball field. We had recently moved to the town, and didn't know that that particular field was a notorious hangout for local tough kids. After the tryout, I was excited that I had done well, and was walking ahead of my dad back to our car when I was approached by a group of bullies. When the leader of the group, a rough-looking nine-or ten-year-old, stepped forward, I knew I was in trouble.

My immediate reaction was relief, knowing my dad was there to protect me, but when I looked in his direction and he made no effort to intercede on my behalf, I realized that I was on my own. I made a mental note to have a serious talk with Dad as soon as this was over. The leader of the group began taunting me and circling me like a vulture. The other kids were encouraging the bully to punch me, hit me, beat me up. I knew enough to hold up my hands in self-defense, but I could tell I was going to have to fight.

1

I put on the so-called "mean face" that I had practiced with my brothers, and told the bully, "I'm not scared of you," even though I was terrified. The bully never moved one inch closer to me, instead continuing to circle. Finally he told his friends that I "wasn't worth it," and even though they were egging him on to fight, he just shrugged and led the group off without ever throwing a punch. I couldn't believe it!

I didn't say one word to my dad all the way to the car, but when we got in, I let him have it. "What were you thinking?" I yelled. "I could have gotten killed!" He assured me that he wouldn't have allowed me to get hurt, and said that it was important for me to learn to stand up for myself. He said that he wouldn't always be there for me in situations like these, so I had to learn how to handle myself.

My dad was also impressed by the "mean face" I had given the bully. He said that it had been enough to convince the bully to back off, and that sometimes that's all it takes. That was the end of our conversation about the incident, but it has stayed with me my whole life.

Almost all children will experience some kind of bullying in their lifetimes, and it may leave life-long scars. Understanding the effecting of bullying is the first step to solving the problem.

First of all, what is bullying? Bullying is *not* the playful horsing around that's part of growing up. Competitive scrapping or good-natured teasing is not to be confused with bullying. According to the Merriam-Webster's dictionary, a bully is categorized as an aggressive person who intimidates or mistreats weaker people. The traditional definition of bullying can expand beyond someone who merely exhibits aggressive behavior. Bullying includes name-calling, making fun of others, spreading nasty rumors, exclusion, and physical aggression. Other definitions of bullying describe it as any deliberate and hostile behavior intended to harm others. For the most part this is true, but I also believe there are circumstances in which a child engages in bullying behavior without it being a conscious decision. For example, a young girl, not realizing the damage it will cause, e-mails a rumor about another schoolmate to all her friends. She doesn't fit in the traditional parameters of a bully according to the dictionary, but she is exhibiting a form of bullying whether she knows it or not.

BULLYING BEHAVIOR

The three basic ways that kids bully each other are verbally, physically, and socially. In my experiences teaching young kids, boys tend to physically bully more than girls, and girls tend to verbally bully more than boys. Social bullying is harder to detect, such as with Internet bullying (cyberbullying), exclusion, ignoring, isolating, and spreading rumors. Although typically girls are associated with this type of bullying, boys sometimes participate in it as well.

There are many common characteristics in children that bully others. Usually, bullies are impulsive, quick to lose their tempers, like to be in control, get frustrated easily, let repressed emotions explode in inappropriate ways, don't have a natural understanding of others' feelings, and tend to have difficulty following rules.

GENDER DIFFERENCES IN BULLYING

In my experiences teaching children that have a history of being bullied, it seems that boys tend to bully physically, whereas girls tend to bully verbally. Boys are more overtly aggressive, and are more likely to resort to pushing, slapping, or hitting. Girls tend to use more indirect forms of aggression, like spreading rumors and excluding others. Additionally, girls outnumber boys when it comes to being the victims of rumors and sexual attacks, both verbal and physical.

2
Bullying Statistics

I've collected some vital statistics* to help everyone understand the seriousness of this problem, and the lasting effects of bullying.

- 80 percent of adolescents report being bullied at some point during their school years.
- 90 percent of children in fourth through eighth grade report being victims of bullying.
- 30 percent of students in grades six through ten are involved in moderate or frequent bullying—as bullies, victims, or both—according to the first national survey on the subject.
- Up to 7 percent of students in eighth grade stay home at least once a month because of bullies.
- Each day, an estimated 160,000 children miss school out of fear of attack or intimidation by other students.
- One out of every ten students who drops out of school does so because of repeated bullying.

*Sources: Bullystoppers.com, Bullying.org, SafeYouth.org, and the National School Safety Center.

- Those who are bullied are five times more likely to be depressed and far more likely to be suicidal.
- The National Educational Association reports that every day in the U.S., 6,250 teachers are threatened with bodily harm, and 260 are physically assaulted.

Bullying is increasingly viewed as a major contributor to youth violence, including homicide and suicide. Case studies of high school shootings have suggested that bullying was a primary factor in many of the incidents.

OTHER STATISTICS:

- The American Justice Department says that one out of every four children will be physically abused by another youth.
- In a recent study, 77 percent of students said they had been bullied mentally, verbally, or physically, and 14 percent of those who were bullied said they experienced severe (bad) reactions to the abuse.
- One out of five children admits to being a bully or doing some bullying.
- 8 percent of students miss one day of class per month for fear of bullies.
- 43 percent of students fear harassment in the bathroom at school.
- 100,000 students carry a gun to school.
- 28 percent of youths who carry weapons have witnessed violence at home.
- A poll of teens ages 12–17 indicated that the majority think violence has increased at their schools.
- Each month, 282,000 students in secondary schools are physically attacked.
- The majority of youth violence occurs on school grounds.
- Every seven minutes, a child is bullied on a playground, with adults intervening 4 percent of the time and peers intervening 11 percent of the time; and 85 percent of the time no one intervenes.

Sources: Bullystoppers.com, Bullying.org, SafeYouth.org, and the National School Safety Center.

LONG-TERM EFFECTS OF BULLYING

Harassment and bullying have been linked to 75 percent of school-shooting incidents, including the fatal shooting at Columbine High School near Littleton, Colorado, and Santana High School in Santee, California. Children who are bullied for long periods of time can become severely emotionally troubled. Long-term bullying affects children's self-esteem and sense of self-worth. It also increases the chance that they will become withdrawn, depressed, insecure, and socially isolated.

BULLYING AND GANGS

In February, 2007, ABC News aired a disturbing report on gangs in America called *Mean Streets*. The report stated that there are 21,000 gangs in America with over 700,000 members. These gangs have grown all across America, and are no longer concentrated in only large cities. Gangs are now recruiting over the Internet in what is called "netbanging." Children can view online recruitment videos where gang leaders explain the advantages of joining their individual gangs, including enticements like money, bling (jewelry), sex, drugs, and guns.

It's a proven fact that teenagers who display bullying tactics as children have a greater probability of winding up participating in illegal activities as well as belonging to violent gangs. Nearly 60 percent of boys whom researchers classified as bullies in grades six through nine were convicted of at least one crime by the age of 24, and 40 percent had three or more convictions by age 24. As parents, we have a moral obligation to take whatever action we can to protect our children from abuse at the hands of these violent gangs, and to keep them from ending up as gang members as well.

3

When Should a Child Fight Back?

When is it acceptable for your child to defend him- or herself? In other words, when is it okay to fight back? Parents have to be able to effectively communicate to their child when it's acceptable to use force and when it's not. For those parents who have enrolled their children in a martial arts program, the instructor is already giving them guidance about when using force is a valid option. For other parents, you will need to rely on common sense.

For example, say a thirteen-year-old, fairly large, and powerfully built bully physically threatens your small, nine-year-old, mild-mannered son. Under these circumstances, fighting back is not a reasonable option unless your child has proper self-defense training. If your son is ever in this situation, encourage him to do everything possible to escape from the bully—including running away. If your son attempts to physically engage this bully when the bully has a clear physical advantage, your son is likely to get hurt. That's not an outcome that we as parents are willing to risk.

MYTH VERSUS FACT

Traditionally, most anti-bullying instruction advocates never using any amount of physical force. Here is a common myth and its refuting "fact."

Myth: "Just stand up for yourself and hit them back."

"Fact": While there are some times when children will be forced to defend themselves, hitting back usually makes the bullying worse and increases the risk for serious physical harm.

Let's discuss this so-called fact. In the above scenario, where the bully has a clear size advantage, this is good advice. However, if the children are close to the same age, weight, height, etc., I don't agree with this premise at all. Let's further examine this "never fighting back" idea, because this is where my book will differ from most other anti-bullying books. As an expert in the martial arts, I have taught thousands of young children to successfully defend themselves against bullies, and not all of them had black belts in the martial arts. Even some of my white belts (beginners) have been able to successfully deal with bullying incidents. I have had students with less than two weeks of instruction who were able to gain the physical skills and self-confidence to handle the bully tormenting them.

For example, after just one lesson, a child can learn how to stop a bully from grabbing him, as in this photo:

Using the strategies and techniques in this book, your child will gain the confidence and skills needed to defend himself against bullies just as my martial arts students have.

A SELF-DEFENSE COURSE FOR YOUR CHILD

Is it acceptable for a parent to allow or encourage their child to physically defend him or herself from a bully attack? When a child is being threatened, I think that it is. Furthermore, I believe that every parent should enroll their child in a self-defense program or martial arts school, especially if he or she is being bullied. Realistically, telling your child to defend himself, without giving him the proper training to do so, is no different than telling your child to play the piano without an instructor. After you work with your child on the self-defense techniques in this book, he will have a much better chance of defending himself against the typical bully.

BULLYING SCENARIOS

Day One

Your twelve-year-old son is confronted by a neighborhood bully close to his age. The bully threatens to hurt your son. Your son attempts to walk away, but the bully doesn't allow it. Next, your son tries to reason with the bully, to no avail. Your son then attempts to lighten the tension by making some witty comments, but the bully isn't buying it. The bully shoves your son and your son just stands there, not wanting to escalate the situation. The bully slaps your son hard across the face, but, not wanting to anger the bully further, your son takes the slap, which is followed by a series of harder slaps, until the bully gets bored. Should your son have just taken the beating, not wanting to risk serious harm, or was blocking the bully's blows a viable reaction?

Day Two

The same bully catches your son on the playground. He tells your son there is nothing he can do to avoid a beating, and then punches your son in the face. Your son's nose starts to bleed, but again, he doesn't want to anger the bully, so he just stands there and takes the abuse. Should your son attempt to defend himself at this point?

Day Three and Beyond

At this point, the bully is confident that your son isn't going to fight back, so it is likely that he will tease or physically attack your son whenever he has the opportunity. Your son knows that he has done nothing to anger the bully, and can't understand why he's being singled out. Barbara Coloroso, author of *The Bully, the Bullied and the Bystander*, sheds some light on this type of incident.

> Bullying is not about anger. It is not a conflict to be resolved; it's about contempt—a powerful feeling of dislike toward someone who is considered to be worthless, inferior, or undeserving of respect. Contempt comes with three apparent psychological advantages that allow kids to harm others without feeling empathy, compassion, or shame. These are: a sense of entitlement, that they have the right to hurt or control others, intolerance towards difference, and a freedom to exclude, bar, isolate, and segregate others.

This bully, who for whatever reason has contempt for your son, feels even more empowered knowing your child is just going to take his abuse. As the frequency and intensity of the beatings increase, it will become too late for your son to start defending himself, even if he wanted to. If your son continues his passive course, not angering the bully further with any reaction, the bully will almost certainly continue the beatings, potentially inflicting incredible pain and suffering. If a child allows himself to be physically abused by a bully, it is likely that the attacks will not stop until someone does something about it. At what point does your son have the right to defend himself with force?

One bullying program that I am aware of suggests that your child should attempt to ask the bully for a hug, which may stop the bully in his tracks. But honestly, real life is so different than the altruistic one we all hope for. Not only do I doubt that this would change a bully's mind about picking on a child, I think that an action like this would almost certainly escalate the bully's attacks. Academic solutions are wonderful in theory, but in the real world, these tactics can get your child hurt even worse. This is why martial arts schools are flooded with young students who want to learn to defend themselves. What I have taught my own children, shown my martial arts students, and am now telling you as parents, is that *no one has the right to put their hands on your child in a harmful way at any time.*

4

The Increase in Bullying in America

Though there have been countless surveys and studies done on bullying, there is unfortunately no single, cohesive reason that we can point to as the underlying cause. We do know that bullying occurs across social, racial, and economic lines. It affects children of all backgrounds, living in all different environments. Bullying happens everywhere and your children are exposed to it on a daily basis. And, unfortunately, it is only increasing. This is simply the reality. Reading this book and learning these basic self-defense techniques will help you and your children deal with this reality, to ensure that your child will be one less victim. But why is bullying on the rise in our society?

MY PERSPECTIVE

Mike Genova's Single Mother

My good friend Mike Genova shared with me his own personal story about growing up in a fatherless home. Mike's mother is no longer with us, but I remember her well, and I personally think she was

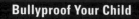

just as much a saint as Mike believed she was. Mike is one of six children, and recalls the many trials and struggles his mother went through in order to raise all of them properly. Mike points out that she couldn't have done it on her own, though, and further explained it this way:

> Imagine a game of tug-of-war. On one side is a single mother. On the other side are all the negative influences impacting your child on a daily basis. Which side has the greatest percentage of winning this battle to control your child's behavior?

A Single Mother's Tug-of-War

No strong male role model
Negative peer pressure
Violence on television and in the movies
Bullies
Guns   ←——————→   MOTHER
Alcohol
Drugs
Sex
Crime
Gangs

These negative forces present overwhelming odds against any well-intentioned single mother trying to raise children on her own.

Genova Family's Tug-of-War

Examine how Mike's mother handled this tug-of-war of life in a different manner.

Negative peer pressure
Violence on television and in the movies   Mother
Bullies   Older Cousins
Guns   Karate Instructor
Alcohol   ←——————→   Male Role Models
Smoking   Grandparents
Drugs   Aunts
Sex   Uncles
Crime   Religious Leaders
Gangs   Sporting Activities

As we can see from this example, Mike Genova's mother had a much better chance of winning this tug-of-war against all the negative influences her children faced. She made the decision to involve her children in karate, team sports, and church, as well as providing other strong male and female influences in their daily lives. She didn't attempt to tackle this tough task on her own, realizing that her children needed a variety of positive role models in their lives, who would reinforce the values she taught them and help to keep them on the right path in life.

Family Dinnertime

Too many households no longer have the simple luxury of eating dinner together as a family. In my generation, dinner was the time when much of the family bonding took place. It was at the dinner table that parents imparted life lessons to their children, such as honesty, integrity, personal responsibility, respect, etc. It was over dinner where parents also instilled their own do's and don'ts in their children's minds, establishing a moral compass for the family to live by. It was also the place where children shared their own personal stories, their dreams, and their fears.

I can still vividly recall an evening when I was ten, sitting at the dinner table and joking with my siblings about some type of construction worker and what he did for a living. My father angrily cut us short and made it painfully clear that we were to show proper respect for any person who worked for a living, regardless of what they did to make ends meet. That was just one of the hundreds of life lessons that molded me into the person I am today. When are the children in today's families learning these valuable lessons? On the way to soccer practice, after being picked up at eight o'clock at night from their dance lessons?

Economic factors today dictate that many parents work longer than eight-hour days now, sometimes working ten- to twelve-hour shifts, which cuts down the amount of time they can spend at home with their children. And for their part, children are involved in karate lessons, soccer, baseball, football, and a host of other activities, making it even harder for families to gather around a dinner table as in the past. I realize times change, and perhaps these changes can be construed as positive trends, but the fact remains that how we govern and monitor our own children has dramatically changed.

Advances in Technology

Families have changed dramatically over the last few decades due to advances in technologies: the Internet, e-mail, cellular phones, etc. (I will discuss this further in Chapter 16.)

Glorification of Violence

There is a strong glorification of and obsession with violence in our society at present. Children are becoming desensitized to violence, with all of the overwhelming displays of it in their daily lives. Unless a child is completely sheltered, he is potentially exposed to visual acts of violence available almost all the time via the Internet, video games, television, movies, and in their own school and personal lives.

John's Story

After one of my recent seminars at a New York school, a man approached and asked me to speak to his teenaged son, John, about his propensity for "extreme," adrenaline-fueled activities. I assumed that John was probably involved in challenging activities that many parents don't approve of, but are quite normal by today's standards, such as bungee jumping, mountain biking, skateboarding, etc. I couldn't have been more wrong.

John bragged about how he and his friends spent their time picking on other kids and starting fights, basically doing anything that would give them an adrenaline rush. Sometimes they would even fight each other with barbed wire, just for fun. As he was telling me this, I noticed many cuts and bruises on his arms. He told me that personal injuries were respected by his peers as a mark of courage. I was taken aback, and glanced over to his dad, who only raised his hands in frustration. My initial reaction was to recommend professional help, but according to John, that would mean that nearly all of his schoolmates needed help as well.

I asked John where he and his friends got the idea to take part in activities where there was such a high chance that they would get hurt. He told me that all of his friends loved to watch reality shows on TV like *Jackass* and *The Wild Boys*. On these shows, the actors participate in incredibly dangerous stunts with a total disregard for personal safety. While I am not drawing correlations between these shows and bullying per se, there is evidence that television shows such as these do impact children's behavior.

Our Children are Becoming Desensitized

It's been reported that our children will view more than 100,000 acts of violence on television by the time they finish grade school. In 2007, most young kids are exposed daily to the harsh, violent realties of the war in Iraq. The casualty and wounded list from the war are reported on the daily news as regularly as sport scores. Acts of violence on TV and in the movies are increasing at an alarming rate, and when the Internet is included, it's easy to deduce why bullying is increasing in our society.

As I previously mentioned, children are now able to view online videos of real-life violence on Web sites such as YouTube, Metacafe and a host of others. In January 2007, the national news televised a homemade web video of a twelve-year-old year girl having her hair pulled and being viciously kicked and punched by a mob of other teen girls. This type of violent video was just one of many available on these sites.

After researching teen fighting and bullying on a few of these popular Web sites, one conclusion I came to is that the bystanders were as responsible for these confrontations as those actually doing the fighting. I viewed a multitude of incidents where the bystanders were encouraging, cheering for, and egging on the fighters, almost in hysteria. Only occasionally, at the end of a long, exhausting fight, would someone attempt to step in to break it up, but that was rare at best.

Mixed Martial Arts

There is a new form of combat gaining wider acceptance today, called mixed martial arts, an increasingly violent, full-contact sparring, where the winner of a match literally knocks his opponent out. There are many associations for this new brand of action, such as UFC, Pride, Extreme Fighting, and Bodog.

In martial arts tournaments in the '70s and '80s, competitors were disqualified for excessive contact. The winner of a point-fighting match was the one who scored the most "controlled points" (kicks or punches) against their opponent. Tournament promoters found it extremely difficult to secure corporate sponsorships because of karate's inherent physical violence. Now, point-fighting tournaments are considered too tame for corporate sponsors, as well as most audiences. Mixed martial arts and its extreme violence has become today's primary spectator sport.

I was recently at a mixed martial arts event and was stunned by the crowd's reaction to the full-contact fights in the arena. Men, women, and children were standing, screaming, and cheering for their favorite fighters with comments like, "Knock him out and kill him!" I felt like I had gone back in time, and was sitting in the Roman Coliseum.

The Martial Arts Child

Many people who have not explored martial arts disciplines have tried to make a case against the martial arts industry for encouraging acts of violence, but this couldn't be further from the truth. Children who are enrolled in martial arts programs go through rigorous physical and mental training. A child enrolled in the martial arts is taught *never to use their skills in an offensive manner*, and respect for one another is the cornerstone of the entire art. Discipline, honesty, and integrity are reinforced in every class.

Zero-Tolerance Policy in Schools

The zero-tolerance policy in schools is a major concern for many. It's my personal opinion that a "one size fits all" solution doesn't work with the myriad of possible bullying situations in classrooms. I realize the intention of the school system is to treat violent situations harshly in an attempt to curtail bullying in schools. But I think a better solution would be to allow schoolteachers the discretion to handle confrontational situations as they see fit.

My recommendation to parents about what to teach their children to do if they are being bullied at school is to think of their child's physical and mental safety first, then deal with the school administrators.

A definition of the term "politically correct" according to the Encarta World English Dictionary is: deliberately inoffensive: marked by language or conduct that deliberately avoids giving offense. We strive as a society not to offend others if possible, but there are times when an aggressive posture must be taken to ensure the safety of your child.

THE SOLUTION

Be the Parent

Take complete charge in determining how your children are raised; be proactive in every facet of their lives and do not allow television, movies, and Web sites to do the parenting for you.

WHO ARE THE BULLIES?

According to expert sources on bullying behavior such as SafeYouth.org and Bullying.com, most bullies were themselves bullied at one time, and are now acting in the same manner. It is commonly believed that bullies hide their feelings of insecurity by acting tough. While this is certainly true at times, in my experiences, bullies tend to be confident, with high self-esteem. Their strong need to dominate others makes them physically aggressive, and they tend to be hot-tempered and impulsive, with a low tolerance for frustration and little empathy for their victims. Of course, there are many different types of bullies, from the bully that attacks verbally or physically to those who aren't aware of their bullying at all.

Male bullies tend to be physically bigger and stronger than female bullies, and get in trouble more often. Most bullies do poorly in school, and as they age, they are more likely to drink and smoke than are their peers.

Discipline

Children whose parents fail to monitor their activities are more likely to engage in bullying behavior. Many "latchkey children" who are left alone most of the time are also at greater risk. Many psychologists believe that children whose parents engage in moderate discipline are less likely to become bullies than children whose parents are either excessively harsh or overly permissive.

KEITH VITALI'S FOUR ACTION STEPS TO DECREASE BULLYING IN AMERICA

As a martial arts instructor, I have been incredibly fortunate to be able to work with thousands of young children, impacting their lives in a positive manner. From these experiences, I believe that the following steps must be taken in order to decrease the amount of bullying in our schools today.

1. Parents Taking More Responsibility
2. Schools Enforcing Anti-Bullying Programs
3. Reshaping the Bully's Behavior
4. Teaching Children How *Not* to Be Victims

Parents Taking More Responsibility

Parents are first in line when it comes to decreasing bullying incidents in our children's lives. Parents are responsible for making sure their children know what bullying is, and how to deal with it.

Teach Your Child Not to Be a Bully

Making sure your child understands that it is always wrong to bully someone who is weaker and more vulnerable, whether by name-calling, cruel teasing, intimidating, threatening, or hitting. And, just as important, make him understand that more subtle forms of bullying are just as wrong: things like spreading rumors, excluding others, encouraging others to bully, or doing nothing to stop a bully in action. Make sure your child understands the harmful, long-term effects that verbal and physical bullying can have on someone.

Share Personal Stories about Bullying in Your Own Life

Telling your child stories of how you were bullied when you were young will have a strong emotional impact, and sharing the lingering emotional effects will leave a long-term impression in his or her mind. Keep in mind, children need to emotionally connect with the lessons you teach them. Don't just tell your child not to pick on others, but teach him why he shouldn't. Use the inspirational stories in this book, or ask your friends to share theirs. This will help these lessons stay with your child, and have a positive impact on their behavior.

Reassure Your Child That You Will Always be There for Him

Make sure your child knows that you will not accept or tolerate anyone bullying him, and that you will do everything in your power to stop it if it ever happens. This lets your child know that he can always come to you immediately if he's suffering at the hands of a bully.

Teach Your Child to Project Confidence and Strength

Bullies are drawn to children who seem weak. Role-play with your child so he is able to speak confidently in front of others. This may be difficult, but give him a lot of encouragement and positive reinforcement as he improves.

Be the Parent

Do not let your child make the rules. You as the parent must decide what's best for your child, and enforce the rules you set. Parents also need to teach their children social survival skills, and, using the lessons in this book, how to stand up for and defend themselves should the need arise.

In addition, parents need to watch for signs of their own child becoming a bully. If you think this may be the case, take drastic measures to radically change your child's bullying mentality, the sooner the better. If the problem is severe, you may need to seek help from a professional, like a child psychologist.

Schools Enforcing Anti-Bullying Programs

There is much that can be done to reduce bullying within our schools. Schools have teachers, administrators, counselors, librarians, janitors, cooks, coaches, and other helpers who could be guarding against bullying, yet bullying persists in almost every school in the nation. What is needed is an adequate training program for teachers to learn how to deal with the different types of bullying situations that kids are faced with on a daily basis. Teachers need to incorporate effective anti-bullying programs into their curricula that will educate students about the harmful effects of bullying. As I have previously discussed, I believe that the zero-tolerance rules should be abolished, returning discretionary powers to the teachers, so they can handle each conflict as they see fit.

This way, schoolchildren will have confidence that their teachers will take appropriate, fair action in the event of a bullying incident.

Reshaping the Bully's Behavior

The third ingredient in reducing bullying is dealing with the bully him- or herself. Early in a child's life, basic morals should be taught, such as compassion, humility, respect for oneself and others, honor, integrity, etc. I recommend that if a parent believes their child is behaving in a bullying fashion, they should be given martial arts training. Of course, martial arts schools are also filled with students seeking to learn how to defend themselves against bullies, but this same training is good for the bully as well. Reprogramming bullying behavior is possible with the right training. Under my instruction, former bullies have turned their lives around and become productive, respectful students, and if I can do this on a local scale, there's no reason it cannot be done nationwide.

Teaching Children How *Not* to be Victims

The final step in reducing bullying in our schools is to teach students how to not become victims. Children need to take personal responsibility and learn how to protect themselves effectively. There will be many times in a child's life when there is no adult supervision and he will have to stand up for himself. Enroll your child in a martial arts program, or work with your child yourself, but give them the necessary tools to defend themselves. That includes all of the lessons in this book, from projecting positive body language, learning assertive communication skills, speaking clearly and confidently, making new friends, and being able to verbally and physically defend themselves.

So what is the answer? In my opinion, continued monitoring in schools for the prevention of bullying incidents is essential, but for dramatic changes to really occur, anti-bullying programs have to be implemented that teach children to respect one another. It will be through the education process that a child will learn what defines a bully, and the damaging effects of their actions. Again, the school should not be the primary source of education on bullying issues; that's the parent's role.

The parents, the schools, the bully, the victim, and all school students need to complement each other in their approach to stopping bullying. With this approach, by the time a child enters middle school, a reduction in bullying incidents should be achieved.

5

How Bullies Choose Their Victims

While there is no single common denominator for the type of child targeted by bullies, a bully will typically search out those who are weaker, smaller, anxious, insecure, cautious, and overtly suffer from low self-esteem. Another child who fits the role of the victim almost automatically is the new kid at school, regardless of his or her personality or physical characteristics. Victims often lack social skills, are isolated from their peers, and rarely defend themselves or retaliate when confronted by bullies. One of the most frequent reasons given for why a particular child has been bullied is that they "didn't fit in."

Here are Some Common Characteristics of Children Who are Targeted by Bullies:

- The new kid at school or in the neighborhood
- Children from different racial backgrounds
- Children from different religious backgrounds

- Children with handicaps or disabilities
- Children who wear glasses
- Children who wear braces
- Children who are overweight
- Children who are underweight
- Children with excessive acne
- The smallest child in a group
- The weakest child in a group
- The tallest child in a group
- The shortest child in a group
- Extremely rich children
- Extremely poor children
- Shy children
- Children who cry easily
- Children who suck their thumbs
- Children who are generally followers
- Children who don't stand up for themselves
- Children who are overtly smart
- Children who play musical instruments
- Children who spend most of their time on the computer
- Younger siblings

As you can see, the list of potential victims represents all kind of children, which is one of the major barriers to preventing bullying among our children. Almost anyone can be singled out as "different," making them more likely to be bullied. The key is that bullying is a learned response, and we need to teach our children from a very young age about the harmful effects of bullying. Most bullies were bullied themselves, and the vicious cycle needs to be stopped.

CHOOSING VICTIMS SUBCONSCIOUSLY

Often, bullies select their victims subconsciously, rather than making a conscious decision to target one child over another. Sometimes the victim is broadcasting signs of weakness, which the bully picks up on. Children who display weak body language transmit signals to the control-minded bully that say *I am someone you can pick on*. Here's one of the analogies I share with my students to give them a better understanding of the way bullies choose their victims. I ask them, *Do you think a bully chooses their victims the following way: A young bully wakes up in the morning, brushes his teeth, gets dressed, and heads to the kitchen for breakfast. His mother is making oatmeal and asks her precious child who he intends to pick on today. The bully responds, "I don't know, I'll think I'll just pick on a red-headed boy today, mom." His mom replies, "Oh, that's nice, dear."* Of course my students laugh and say that they know that's not how bullies choose their victims.

SHOPPING-FOR-A-SHIRT THEORY

Then how does a bully choose his victims? Here's one theory I share with my students: A mother takes her young boy to the mall to buy him some clothes. The boy knows he needs a new shirt. He's basically clueless as to what kind of shirt he's looking for, but he's sure he'll know it when he sees it. This is similar to how a bully chooses his victim. At the store, he looks at shirt after shirt until he spots one he likes. Again, he really doesn't know what he's looking for until one of the shirts appeals to him. Similarly, a bully sitting in class most likely has no particular victim in mind until someone sends him signals. These signals are usually signs of weakness demonstrated through body language.

For example, the teacher asks the young boy in the back of the room, Paul, to introduce himself to the class. He stands up and begins to speak softly, when the teacher interrupts and invites him to come up to the front of the classroom. Paul is clearly nervous and uncomfortable about doing so, but he shyly makes his way up to the front. He begins to stutter, speaking in a low, unsure voice. Knowing that he's blowing it, he begins to fidget, moving side to side unconsciously, then raising a hand to his mouth. His words stop making sense, and kids begin laughing out loud. Somewhere in the class, one of the classmates is staring out the window, bored with everything, until he hears the laughter of the others. The weak traits coming from the speaker in the front of the class are picked up by the bully as if by radar. The bully has now subconsciously found his victim.

RACIALLY MOTIVATED BULLYING

One of the most difficult issues to write about is racially motivated bullying. Parents of all races have legitimate concerns about the safety of their children who are in a racial minority at their school. Children who bully will use any excuse to control and humiliate others, and a different racial background is just another personality difference for them to exploit.

What should parents do if their children are in a racial minority? First, at the beginning of the school year, make sure to meet as many of the teachers and administrators who have a daily impact on your child as possible. Share your concerns and ask what steps are being taken to keep your child safe outside of the classroom. Do not ask in a threatening manner, or one that could be perceived as bigoted, but explain that you are concerned that your child may be singled out and bullied for being different. Ask how you can assist the teacher, or how you can help out at school, perhaps by carpooling, organizing special events, joining the PTA, etc. In this way you will ensure that you are not just a faceless parent, but one who will be respected and remembered. The teacher will be more likely to pay special attention to your child and notify you if there is any problem. Your job as a parent is to make sure that the authority figures in your child's school consider the safety of your child a priority.

One of the fears students have is that nothing will be done to stop them from being bullied, which is one reason they don't tell their teacher. According to one study by Craig and Pepler in 1997, bullying is often hidden from teachers. Teachers' lack of awareness is evident in playground observations in which teachers intervened to stop only *one in twenty-five* bullying episodes.

6

If Your Child is Being Bullied

Unless your child tells you about it, how can you tell if your child is being bullied? There are certain signs that children exhibit when they're under stress from bullying. This chapter will explain what these signs are, how to spot them, and what you can do about it.

In *The Bully, the Bullied, and the Bystander*, Barbara Coloroso says not to expect your child to come running home and confess that they are being bullied, something many children consider shameful. Often they will not tell their parents because they are afraid of reprisals. But there are certain symptoms that should make you suspicious. These include a variety of characteristics that you may not be aware of, unless you're paying careful attention.

Questions to Ask Yourself to Determine Whether your Child is Being Bullied

- Are they not sleeping soundly each night?
- Are they complaining of frequent headaches or stomachaches?
- Are they losing their appetite?

- Are they exhibiting signs of depression?
- Are they going directly to the bathroom when they get home from school, possibly to avoid a conversation?
- Are they asking for or stealing money from you?
- Do they want to be left alone or withdraw from friends and family?
- Have they begun to lose interest in sports or playing with others?
- Do they make up excuses not to go to school?
- Are they taking a different route home from school or the park?
- Have their grades dropped?
- Do they have injuries they are trying to hide, like black eyes, scratches, cuts, or bruises?
- Do they come home with missing or torn items such as books, backpacks, or clothes?

One caution here is not to confuse teasing or playing games with being bullied. Be clear about what is going on with your child. If he acts like things are just fine, they probably are. But if he can't sleep at night, hides in the bathroom, will not touch his food, or refuses to go to school, there is most likely a problem, and the faster and more decisively you deal with it, the better.

WHAT YOU CAN DO

If you think your child is being bullied, try not to be too direct or accusatory with your questions. Ask how school is going, or if anything happened on the way home or on the bus. Then you can gradually bring the conversation around by asking if they know of any bullies at their school and how they feel about it. The best advice I can offer is to stay calm and be a good listener. Allow your child to tell you their side of the story at their own pace and then gently tell him or her that together, you will figure out what should be done.

Many children are scared about reprisals or reprimands if they tell on the bully. I continuously stress that kids should not feel reluctant to go to their parents if they're having bullying issues. Most of the time, bullying doesn't just go away, but escalates, so proactive measures must be taken to protect your child. Make sure that your child is comfortable talking to you and knows that you are on their side.

Parents Have Superpowers

"Every parent is essentially a black belt with superpowers when their child is in trouble," I tell my students, "What do you think would happen if your little sister, for example, was at the mall and managed to slip away from your mother—and an evil person grabbed her and started to run out the door with your sister under his arm? Do you think your mother would just stand there screaming for help? No, your mother would turn into one of the indestructible monsters you've seen in the movies. She would be out the door, beating that evil person to the ground with her shoes or whatever she could grab, so she could get her daughter back." The kids laugh, but get the message: Your parents want to protect you. Don't be afraid to talk to them, because they absolutely want to help.

TALKING TO A TEACHER OR PRINCIPAL

Here is an example of how I handled a situation in which one of my students—let's call him Bob—was worried about telling his parents he was being bullied at school. Bob reluctantly confided in me that he was being picked on and didn't know how to handle it. He said that he told his teacher about the bully, but the bullying persisted when adults weren't around. I persuaded him to tell all of this to his parents, which he did. I then invited all of them into the office so we could develop a game plan for dealing with the problem.

As a martial arts instructor, I have dealt with many similar situations, and I realized that parents might not know how to handle these problems any more than their children do. With Bob, I volunteered to make the initial attempt to solve the bullying issue, and his parents consented. I started by approaching the principal at Bob's school. Here is what I said.

"Hi, Mrs. Smith, I just wanted to call and introduce myself. I'm a martial arts instructor in the area, and I'm available for any talk, self-defense demonstration, or whatever you might want in the way of child safety issues. Just let me know if I can offer my services in any way."

Mrs. Smith thanked me, and after some small talk, I explained my real reason for calling. "I'd like to ask for your help with something. One of my students, Bob, is a fifth-grader in your school. He confessed to me that he's being picked on by another child in his class. He said that he's mentioned it to his teacher, but the bullying has continued. Bob is such a good student, and he doesn't know how to handle this situation. Is there anything you can do?" The principal assured me that she would have a talk with Bob's teacher, and she did so. The bully was soon called into her office and persuaded to stop picking on Bob.

A week later, I sent the principal a card, letting her know how much I appreciated her immediate action. You, as a parent, have to act in the same fashion. Be courteous, but be aggressive in your actions to stop your child from being targeted by a bully or bullies. Keeping a cool head and always following up with a courteous phone call, e-mail, or letter to the principal or teacher will go a long way, and will secure their willingness to help out with any future issues that might arise. Act quickly when you see a dramatic change in your child's behavior, take action, and don't assume that they're just kids and will work it out on their own. Children have plenty to worry about without having to deal with bullying issues by themselves.

ASKING AN OLDER CHILD TO TALK TO THE BULLY

Each bullying situation is unique, and my strategies vary with every situation. Sometimes I will ask an older student to help out. For this, I usually choose a high-ranking martial artist who considers it a privilege to help out a younger schoolmate. The older student will be trained in exactly how to handle the situation and what to say.

Upon finding the bully, my upper-belt student explains that the bully's target is a friend of his, and that he would consider it a personal favor if they would leave his friend alone. Before the bully can respond with some type of denial, my student asks, in a very assertive manner, "Do

you understand what I am saying?" Once the bully says he understands, my student smiles and says, "That's great. I'm really glad we had this conversation. I'll be keeping my eye on you."

This strategy has worked plenty of times. If you want to try a similar method, I recommend using an older schoolmate or a neighborhood friend to persuade the bully to stop harassing your child. Use good judgment here—you don't want to turn your operative into a bully himself—but the goal is for him to make it very clear that there will be consequences if the bullying persists.

STEPS TO TAKE IF YOUR CHILD IS BEING BULLIED

Trust Your Child

If your child confesses that's he's being bullied, trust that he's telling you the truth. It could be very emotionally damaging to your child if you don't believe him. Next, make it extremely clear to him that bullying is wrong and you're not going to tolerate it. Again, most kids go through some amount of bullying in their lives, so reassure him that he's not the problem and there's nothing wrong with him.

Take Immediate Action

First, assess the situation. If the bullying is advanced or very serious, or if it has resulted in serious physical or emotional harm to your child, report it immediately to the appropriate authorities. This will most likely be your child's teacher, the bully's teacher, or the principal.

Avoidance

If the bullying is not yet very serious, there are many ways that you and your child can attempt to stop it. First, if it's possible, tell your child to try to avoid the bully, and encourage him to make new friends so he is not always on his own. Bullies are much less likely to target a member of a group than someone who is by himself.

Stand Up to the Bully

If avoidance doesn't work, or is not an option, encourage your child to stand up to the bully—within reason. Convey to him that he shouldn't allow anyone to harass him or take his possessions. Also tell him that by giving in to the bully's demands, he will not discourage the bully from continuing their torments. If your child is not properly trained in how to stand up to a bully, however, he could potentially get hurt. Be careful recommending this course, and make sure your child gets the proper instructions and training before taking any action.

Teach Defensive Strategies

Role playing is a way to teach your child different strategies on how to handle bullies. See the section on "verbal comebacks" later in this book for more on this.

Display Assertive Body Language

Make sure your child knows that it's important for him to try to remain calm when approached by a bully, and not allow the bully the pleasure of knowing that he's affecting your child emotionally. Teach your child to project confidence instead of displaying weak body language that will draw a bully's attention. Some ways to convey assertive body language are: stand tall, speak loudly and clearly, don't fidget, and make direct eye contact.

Reinforce Your Child's Confidence

It is normal for your child to be scared about standing up to a bully. Be sure to calm his anxieties, and continuously build up his self-esteem by reviewing his past successes and accomplishments. Let him know that you believe in him, and you know he is up to this challenge.

Of course, I strongly recommend that you enroll your child in karate or another type of self-defense course. Such programs stress mental discipline and self-control, along with self-defense, and will help to prepare your child both mentally and physically for a possible confrontation.

Should You Call the Bully's Parents?

Most specialists in the field, myself included, recommend *not* calling the bullying child's parents except as a last resort. Parents never want to hear negative accusations leveled at their child, and tend to be defensive. Also, your child is likely to find this type of action extremely embarrassing.

There are certain situations, however, when calling the other child's parents can be the right decision. When I was in eighth grade, my best friend Jimmy and I got in a tussle after school. Jimmy and I exchanged heated words, and the next thing I knew, Jimmy punched me in the nose and we started to fight. While I can't remember the particulars of the fight itself, I vividly remember coming home the next day to find Jimmy and his parents sitting with my parents in our living room. It was Jimmy's parents who had called mine and, knowing that Jimmy and I were good friends, they wanted to figure out what was going on. We all talked about what had happened, and the conversation ended with Jimmy and I shaking hands. While it was embarrassing at the time, I believe our parents' actions helped us to reconcile quickly. We never fought again after that, and remain great friends to this day.

The point here is that every situation is different, which is why it is so important to get as much information as you can from your child. Then you can assess the situation, and take whatever action you deem appropriate to put an end to the conflict.

7

If Your Child Is the Bully

There are many theories as to why bullies act the way they do, usually beginning with lessons they might have learned at home at the hands of their parents or siblings. Most bullies were bullied themselves, and now are re-creating the same scenarios, but this time, they are the aggressors. Sometimes children who bully others think of themselves as superior. In other cases, they act this way to cover up emotional pain, insecurity, or feelings of inadequacy.

Just as there are characteristics common to most victims, there are symptoms that bullies tend to exhibit as well. If your child is exhibiting any of the characteristics discussed in this chapter, they need to be seriously addressed.

COMMON CHARACTERISTICS OF BULLIES

- Seeking attention while being emotionally detached
- Acting like they are superior to other children

- Picking on younger or weaker siblings
- Attempting to dominate others
- Hurting other children when there are no parents or authority figures around
- Insisting that their needs come first
- Disregarding other children's feelings
- Using other children to get what they want
- Finding it difficult to accept responsibility for their actions
- Showing no remorse when they have hurt others
- Seeking to acquire or maintain social status by decreasing others' standing

ATHLETES WHO BULLY

There are also bullies who are not social outcasts, and don't fit the typical characteristics of a bully: overly confident, controlling athletes. The athlete that acts as a bully does so to control and dominate others as a means to gaining social status or popularity. These individuals often have more latitude to commit their injustices without repercussions.

VERBAL BULLIES

Verbal harassment is more than twice as common as physical bullying, and it occurs across all ethnic groups and income brackets. The most common form of verbal bullying is name-calling. Children call each other names for many reasons: It could be the color of their skin, their looks, their size, or a hundred different reasons why one child feels they must put another child down. Normally, victims are shy and display insecurities and low self-esteem, as well as being smaller or weaker than average.

We have all heard the old adage, "Sticks and stones may break my bones, but words will never hurt me." Unfortunately, this is not even close to the truth. Verbal bullying can be much more traumatic and emotionally damaging than physical bullying, and children know this instinctively. When speaking to a group about bullying, I always ask my audience which hurts more: verbal or physical bullying. Almost every child agrees that verbal bullying is far worse. Being punched, shoved, or tripped might hurt physically, but the pain usually subsides after a short time. Not to trivialize physical bullying at all, but verbal bullying often results in long-term emotional problems that don't heal so easily.

CYBERBULLIES

In the twenty-first century, a new kind of bullying has emerged, called *cyberbullying*. The website wikipedia.org defines cyberbullying as "bullying and harassment by use of electronic devices though means of e-mail, instant messaging, text messages, blogs, mobile phones, pagers, and websites." This often anonymous form of bullying allows children to use technology to harm other children.

According to Parry Aftab, executive director of wiredsafety.org, "Because [cyberbullying] can be anonymous, there's no fear of detection. Even if you identify yourself, you don't see people's reactions and realize you have gone too far." How common is cyberbullying? According to wiredsafety. org, 90 percent of middle-school students have had their feelings hurt over the Internet, and 75 percent of children have read something negative about another student online. Even worse, only 15 percent of the parents polled knew what cyberbullying was.

There are unfortunately many different ways a cyberbully can harm others. For example, a bully could use her cell phone to take a photo of another child in an embarrassing or compromising situation, and upload the photo onto her blog or e-mail it to her friends. Another cyberbullying method is to intimidate another child by to sending a cruel e-mail or one that threatens physical harm. The different ways of using technology to harm another child are limited only by the bully's imagination.

WHAT CAN PARENTS DO?

Monitoring your child's Internet and cell phone use is the easiest and most effective solution. If you find that your child is actively participating in cyberbullying, then act accordingly. Take away his phone or computer privileges, inflict some fitting type of punishment, and have him take responsibility for his actions, possibly by apologizing to those he has harmed. If your child is the target of cyberbullying, act quickly to protect him.

With all of the new advances in digital technology, it's getting to the point where children are more computer savvy than most of their parents. In addition to staying on top of your child's activities on their computer, do your best to educate yourself about the kinds of technology your child is using, so that you will be better equipped to help them or help them change their behavior, if the need arises.

According to a February, 2007, article in *Parade Magazine* by Rosalind Wiseman, educators and state legislators from Florida to Oregon are trying to incorporate anti-cyberbullying legislation into new bills. This legislation would allow school officials to intervene in incidents that occur away from school, if the activity can be proven to impact a child's learning environment. This certainly sounds impressive, but it remains to be seen if these bills will even pass, let alone help to effect drastic changes. In the meantime, continue to be vigilant in your awareness of your child's technological activities, so that you will be able to help or protect him if necessary.

I fully realize that monitoring your child's activity over the Internet is a tough task, but one you as a parent are going to have to perform. It may also cause a rift at times between you and your child, especially if he believes you're not giving him his own space, or the independence to live his own life. I'm a parent, so I've heard it all as well, but I made a conscious decision to act as parent first, and a friend second, and I suggest you do the same. Sometimes, it's hard making tough decisions for your child, but that's what parenting calls for.

Sharing Personal Stories with Your Child

Informing kids about the harmful effects of bullying is another major key to defeating the problem. Once children gain a better understanding of the consequences of bullying, it's easier for them to

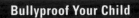

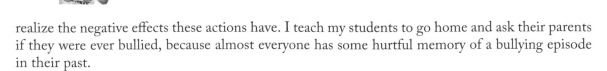

realize the negative effects these actions have. I teach my students to go home and ask their parents if they were ever bullied, because almost everyone has some hurtful memory of a bullying episode in their past.

My Mother's Bullying Story

My own mother told me about the time one of her own schoolmates made fun of her in front of the class because her parents couldn't afford new shoes. She remembered how all the other girls laughed at her, and how those caustic remarks damaged her self-esteem. My mother doesn't remember many details from her early school years, but she vividly remembers that one embarrassing, hurtful experience. The fact that she shared this episode with my siblings and me made each of us more sensitive about how we treated others. Hopefully, sharing your own stories with your child will leave the same type of impression on them.

My role as an instructor was not only to teach young kids how to handle specific bullying situations but also to educate and inform them about the harmful effects of bullying in general, to prevent them from doing any bullying in the future.

SOLUTION

Let your child know that under no circumstances should they allow others to verbally abuse him in any fashion. If the school system doesn't do anything about it, meet with the teachers yourself; if still there is no action, then it's time to meet with their superiors.

8

The Martial Arts Edge

I realize that I'm concentrating much of my focus on the martial arts methods of imposing discipline and respect for others, but that's because of the tremendous success martial artists all over the world have been able to accomplish.

I have personally taught martial arts to students at every age level, including elementary, middle school, high school, and college. I was fortunate to even have my first book, *Beginning Karate*, used as one of the textbooks at the University of South Carolina. Whenever I do demonstrations on self-defense and beginning martial arts at schools, teachers have the same response after watching me interact with children: "I wish we as teachers could do what you are able to do."

They are referring to the way I command discipline and respect from my students. Every student in my classes must act respectfully toward me and the other students and be extremely disciplined, or the student is not allowed to participate.

Martial arts are viewed by most children as being "cool," and are highly regarded in almost every segment of society, which makes our jobs easier when it comes to working with young children. A martial artist is considered to be someone who can adequately defend himself in any situation, and who exhibits positive character traits such as respect, discipline, and integrity. This allows martial arts instructors to influence and mold minds in a positive manner.

Martial arts schools have a definite advantage over school institutions as well as other leadership organizations because there are simply no other institutions designed specifically to teach discipline and respect the way that martial arts schools do. Every single class in every martial arts school in the world begins in the same way, with the students standing at attention. This simple exercise in discipline is much harder than you might think for many students, especially those with high energy. Once the class is perfectly lined up and still, a simple bowing ritual takes place. The students bow to their instructor, expressing their respect for him or her, and then the instructor returns the bow as a sign of respect to the students. From the moment class begins, a formality of discipline is expected and required.

TRANSFORMING ONE DELINQUENT

In one of my after-school karate programs, I had a student who tested my limits immediately. Before class started, I introduced myself to the students sitting on the floor. I noticed some children in the back of the room were giggling and causing a disturbance. I walked over and saw that one child was sniffing glue without even trying to hide it from me! Calmly, I asked him for the glue, and when he gave it to me, I threw it as hard as I could against the back wall. All of the students jumped, and right off the bat, they realized I wasn't the librarian. I could have sent this young, misguided boy to the principal's office for disciplinary action, but I realized he wanted to take karate for a reason, and perhaps it was to better himself. I decided to give him a chance and see if I could help straighten him out.

I ordered all of the students to get to their feet and stand at attention, using a voice as harsh and loud as a drill sergeant's. This startled them and they quickly complied, standing on the marks I had placed on the floor. I let them know that under no circumstances was I going to tolerate behavior like this in my class. I told them to stand there with their hands at their sides and not to utter one single word or move an inch. I told them that they were to address me as Mr. Vitali, and to answer me with a respectful "yes" or "no, sir" when I asked them any questions. I asked them if they understood this nonnegotiable policy, and they yelled in unison, "Yes, sir!"

After that I eased up, smiling and telling them to relax, allowing them to move slightly, but still remain on their marks. I knew that before I could win these kids over, I would have to earn their respect.

I had the children introduce themselves, and made it a point to say something positive about each one. Next, I explained to them that at the beginning and end of each class, we bowed to one another to show our respect. We all bowed, and the class began. In just these few minutes, I had established discipline and respect. Here's what I offered each of them next that's important to share with the reader. I offered each of them *hope*.

I told the students that if they came to class regularly and gave me 100 percent effort, their lives would completely change. I told them that I would turn each one of them into Superman. I reminded them that Superman's real name is Clark Kent, and in everyday life, Clark Kent is well-mannered, respectful, disciplined, honest, and caring. "When does he change into Superman?" I asked the students. They laughed and replied, "When he's in danger or needs to save someone." I explained that if they gave me their best, I would turn each and every one of them into Superman as well. In their daily lives, they would behave just like Clark Kent, but if and when the time came to defend themselves, they would be able to turn themselves into someone as powerful and confident as Superman.

I was offering them hope that their lives could change. I chose the young boy who had been sniffing glue to come up front and help me lead the class in stretching exercises. I emphasized that I was there to make leaders out of each and every of them, and I started with this misguided boy.

Over time, I watched the students change right in front of my eyes. Every one of them came to class and did their best. They took on leadership qualities in class, helping each other, trying their hardest, and showing proper respect for each other and myself. The discipline and skill level they displayed at the year-end demonstration in front of the school amazed the entire student body, as well as the administration. I later learned that the reason these kids made such a good impression among the teachers was that they had been sent to me because of disciplinary problems. Now, these kids were the shining stars at their school.

TRANSFORMING ALL THE DELINQUENTS

Perhaps, that's what's needed in our schools today: boldness, compulsory discipline, and respect for others.

Teachers aren't the culprits here. I realize that their hands are tied by strict rules governing what they can and can't do. Discipline needs to be administered by fair, commonsense measures, but it does need to be enforced if children are going to learn proper respect for each other. Showing one another proper respect is one key ingredient to reducing bullying behavior.

Teaching students to act respectfully must be carefully done. Respect has to be earned—not demanded. One might think that I was a strict disciplinarian when I taught my students, but today's standards are much more lax than when I was a student. My own instructor, John Roper, taught me under the strictest discipline possible, similar to a young soldier at a boot camp. My slightest infraction would caused me to have to do a hundred push-ups. Even though John was a great instructor and remains a good friend today, my classmates and I respected him primarily out of fear. That's just how martial arts programs were structured in the '70s.

I'm certainly not suggesting that that type of discipline be initiated in our school systems. While this military type of discipline does work, it is not the best method. Most, if not all, students will resent and resist this approach, and many will drop out of school rather than deal with it.

USING POSITIVE REINFORCEMENT

I have always tried not to be overbearing or extremely strict, preferring instead to use positive reinforcement. For example, a young girl, let's call her Mary, is in class trying her hardest to execute a basic karate punch, but she is aiming too high. If I correct Mary in front of the entire class with a harsh, loud comment such as, "Mary, you are punching too high, that is not how it's done!" she will be embarrassed and most likely feel bad. Perhaps the reason she enrolled in my martial arts school in the first place was because she had poor self-esteem. If I correct her harshly in front of all her classmates, I stand the chance of tearing her self-esteem down even further. Instead, I walk over and say something positive about her efforts, perhaps mentioning how hard she is trying, and then I physically correct her punch with my hands. After that, I commend her once again, telling her that she's doing a great job. This way, Mary beams with pride, knowing that I'm pleased by her efforts, and tries even harder to correct her punch. This was the teaching philosophy I used for my entire career as an instructor and it generated incredible results. I am extremely proud of the thousands of gifted students that I've had the honor of teaching, many of whom went on to excel in national martial arts tournaments.

Here is another example. A young boy, Jack, timidly enters my class fifteen minutes late. Jack is clearly extremely nervous and embarrassed about being late, expecting to be reprimanded in front of the entire class. If I punish him for being late, most likely all I will accomplish is to damage his self-esteem and confidence.

First of all, the little boy didn't drive to class, so how could it be his fault? Secondly, I always appreciate my students showing up to class, even late. Here's how I handled this situation to ease Jack's anxieties. As soon as he stepped on the mat, I smiled and let him know that I was glad to see him. During class, I approvingly tapped him on his shoulder or helped him to retie his karate belt. It is important to touch him, in an appropriate manner, because touch is essential to developing trust and respect. This reinforces that I am glad he's in my class, and he knows that he has pleased me. Feeling relaxed and approved of, Jack tries his hardest and has a great class.

What if all schools taught their students with the same philosophy, positive reinforcement, that I had so much success with in teaching martial arts? I believe that if a child is repeatedly singled out in class in front of other classmates for doing something incorrectly, he becomes embarrassed and humiliated. This child stands the chance of either turning into a bully, if he's angered enough and decides to take it out on some other child, or becoming withdrawn and unsure, a prime target for bullying.

PARENTS' ONE-TIME RULE AND PERSONAL RESPONSIBILITY RULE

The Parent's One-Time Rule and the Personal Responsibility Rule are two important lessons I taught my students, whether they were having bullying issues or not. Both are simple to do and produce phenomenal results. These programs emphasize respect for others and taking responsibility for one's actions.

Parent's One-Time Rule

This rule stated that whenever a child was asked to do something by his or her parent—clean your room, make your bed, take out the trash—the child was required to obey their parent's request the very first time, and to respond to their parent with a respectful reply. I handed out a sheet to each student, which they would to give to their parents to fill out. At the end of each week, the parents had to return the Parent's One-Time Rule sheet, signed, stating that their child had complied all week long. Then I called each child up to the front of the class and verbally rewarded them for their achievement, building their self-esteem, and gave them a green stripe to be taped to their karate belts. Without at least four green stripes on their belt, students were not eligible to test for promotion to a higher belt.

> In no time at all, students were responding respectfully to their parents and complying with their requests, all the time. Acting respectfully became second nature to them.

Of course, parents absolutely loved this! Many of the parents told me that for the first time, their children were actually listening without complaining, and doing what was asked of them without having to be told several times.

Often, parents need another adult to act as a positive influence in their child's life, because kids have a natural (or unnatural) tendency to listen to others more than to their parents. Including a similarly minded adult in your own children's lives—an uncle, a grandmother, or any other adult that they respect—will reinforce the lessons and values that you teach them.

The Parent's One-Time Rule can be implemented by anyone. If you are trying this with your child, come up with your own creative rewards when they comply, like taking them on a trip to get ice cream, or letting them stay up late one night. The goal is to build a solid foundation of respect early in the child's life. You might also want to consider having these rules come from another trusted adult, especially if it doesn't work at first.

Too often, parents aspire to be their child's best friend and give in too easily. I was guilty of this as well. My daughter Jennifer would just smile, and I would give in to her demands, no matter what they were. My son, Travis, used a different ploy. Every time I began to discipline him, he would fall to the ground and reenact my death scene from the movie I starred in, *Revenge of the Ninja*. My son's acting at nine years old was as bad as my actual acting in the film, and his witty satire of my poor acting performance continuously got him off the hook. I would have to turn my back on him or leave the room, because I didn't want him to see me laughing while I was supposed to be administering some type of punishment. The problem is that every time I let him off the hook with a simple warning, he escaped knowing that he had gotten the best of me.

With both of my children, I had to learn an important lesson, one that every parent must learn: *Be the parent.* When you need to discipline your child, stay firm, speak clearly, and follow through. Otherwise, your children will never learn to respect and obey you.

If your seven-year-old wakes up in the morning and tells you that he doesn't feel like going to school, of course you respond, "That's nice, dear, now get your behind out of bed and get ready for school." You know what's best for him—he's only seven. But what do you say when your child wants to quit taking piano lessons, swimming, soccer, baseball, karate classes, etc? Normally, parents don't want to force children to participate in activities they're not enjoying. I agree, but remember that quitting too easily early on in life becomes habit-forming. *You* need to make these decisions, not your child, or at least you need to make them together.

As a child, I wanted to quit swimming lessons just a week after I started. My mother's response was, "You asked to take the lessons and I'm not going to let you quit. You need to learn that when you start

something, you finish it." I've lived with that philosophy my whole life. Reinforcing positive, respectful behavior in your child will definitely lower the risk that your child will become a bully in the future.

Implementing the Parent's One-Time Rule, especially with children who have tendencies to dominate and disrespect others, was one of the key ingredients to my successes in changing their behavior patterns. It took time, but over the course of their training, I saw troubled, mixed-up children grow into mature young men and women.

The Personal Responsibility Rule

This is the second rule I implemented with my students. Each child was given a second form, The Personal Responsibility Rule sheet, to be given to their parents and returned, signed, along with the Parent's One-Time Rule sheet. This rule states that each child is required to do things around the house—clean up their room, set the table, brush their teeth—without being told to do so by their parents. Once the child had completed ten of these tasks, their parents would sign the form and return it to me. This time, each student would be brought up in front of the class and rewarded with a blue stripe on their belt. As with the green stripes, a minimum of four blue stripes were required in order to test for promotion to the next level. The parents of my students were ecstatic. Not only were their kids responding to their demands the very first time they were asked, they were also acting respectfully, and taking the initiative to do things on their own. Their children, some for the first time, were taking personal responsibility, helping out around the house, and doing it all with a smile. These acts were forced at first, but became habits in just a few months.

Again, try this at home with your child, especially if you believe he is following the path to becoming a bully. Both of these programs help to turn the troublemaker into a productive, respectful kid. This will also help your child develop a sense of accomplishment, giving him more confidence in life.

PARENT'S ONE-TIME RULE—Acting Respectfully
The very first time your parents ask you to do something, you are required to answer them with "Yes, sir (or father)" or "Yes ma'am (or mother)" and then do what they have asked. This certificate entitles _____ to a _____ for listening to your parents and being respectful.

PERSONAL RESPONSIBILITY RULE—Personal Responsibility
Without having to be told by your parents, you are required to perform ten responsible actions around the house this week.
Examples: Make your bed; pick up your toys, clear the table.
1._____
2._____
3._____
4._____
5._____
6._____
7._____

8._____

9._____

10._____

This certificate entitles _____ to a _____ for taking personal responsibility.

BULLYING STORIES

There are hundreds of books, television shows, and movies focusing on the negative effects of bullying, but I want to share some inspirational stories in which a negative bullying experience ended with a positive outcome.

How One Kind Act Saved a Life

Carl was walking home from middle school one day, carrying his books. A group of young bullies came over to Carl and began taunting and demeaning him. Then one of the bullies reached over and knocked the books out of Carl's hands, and everyone in the group laughed.

Stanley, a schoolmate of Carl's, interceded. Stanley stopped the bullies from further harassing Carl, and then helped him pick up his books. Stanley introduced himself to Carl, and reassured him that everything would be okay. The two boys grew up to be best friends.

Years later, Stanley sat in attendance watching Carl gave his summa cum laude graduation speech at his university. The once shy, intimidated boy had grown up, and was now a well-adjusted, confident young man graduating number one in his class. At the end of the speech, Carl said that he wanted to thank one special person in the audience, someone who, he felt, was responsible for Carl making it to where he was today.

He then told the story about that day back in middle school when the bullies had picked on him. He recalled how miserable he had been then, feeling like he had nothing to live for. He told the audience that when the bullies stopped him, he had been on his way home to commit suicide, and had already written a suicide note to leave for his parents.

He then recounted how one courageous boy had interceded on his behalf, stopped the bully's taunts, and shown him some kindness, and that the two had grown up to be best friends. He closed by saying that his dear friend had never known the full story until now, but that Stanley's kindness on that day had saved Carl's life.

School Bullying Story

One of my students—we'll call him Chris—was in eighth grade when a local reform school for troubled kids was merged into his middle school, to see if the problem children could interact safely with others. Immediately, small gangs began intimidating and threatening students. A group of students would approach their victims and stare them down. If any other student looked any of the gang members in the eye, they usually responded by saying, "Who you looking at? Were you eye-ballin' me?" Their strategy was to intimidate everyone around them.

Chris was sitting on the bleachers during a school rally when one of these small gangs approached him. They surrounded him and began their verbal taunting. He decided not to back down, which they took as on offensive gesture. They warned him that they would get him later. Later that day, while Chris was in class, one of the bullies started yelling at him while his teacher was speaking, interrupting the class. Chris tried to ignore the bully, but even when the teacher told him to be quiet, the bully continued yelling. Chris told the bully to back off, but the bully approached him, trying to start a physical fight. Fortunately, Chris was a black belt, and when the bully attacked him, he was able to take the bully down and regain control of the situation. By this time, the principal had arrived.

Chris and the bully were both suspended for fighting because their school had a zero-tolerance policy. I spoke with Chris after his suspension, allowing him to explain his actions. He said that the bullying at his school had been going on for some time and the teachers were not addressing the situation. I asked Chris why he had resorted to violence with the bully, and he told me that he had had no other reasonable choice. The teacher and the other students were doing nothing to intervene. Chris's only two choices were to take a beating or to stand up for himself. He told me that if he hadn't responded the way he did, he potentially could have been bullied the entire year, but that now he knew that no one was going to harass him anymore.

It was fortunate that Chris knew how to stand up for himself, and that no weapons were involved in this situation.

Mike Genova's Playground Bullying Story

I asked my good friend, martial arts expert Mike Genova, to share one of his own personal bullying stories.

When Mike was twelve, he went to a nearby basketball court to play ball. He didn't know anyone at the playground, so he waited his turn to join a pickup game. One of the boys told him that if he wanted to play, he would have to fight a boy named Billy first. Mike asked who Billy was, and the largest member of the group stepped forward. In one quick martial arts move, Mike took the larger boy down.

After that, they never asked another kid to fight someone before joining in a game with them, and Mike is still friends with all of the boys he met that day—including Billy

John Kreng's Bullying Story

Here is a bullying story from John Kreng, another associate of mine who has a black belt.

"When I first went to junior high school, I was afraid for my life, because so many of the kids were bigger and tougher than I was. And I was one of only a handful of Asian kids at the school, in a predominately Caucasian neighborhood, during the height of the U.S. involvement in Vietnam. I was verbally assaulted or physically challenged on an almost daily basis. The solution for me was to take martial arts lessons to protect myself. Being the only son of a single parent (my father died right before my first birthday), my mother could only afford to pay for the classes offered by the YMCA, which were in aikido.

At twelve, my testosterone was getting the better of me, and an esoteric martial art like aikido wasn't something I could easily understand and apply to my daily situation. I desperately wanted to kick and punch in a karate class like my hero Bruce Lee, but beggars cannot be choosers. And as it turns out, the lessons I learned during those three years continue to serve me to this day.

My Japanese sensei was an unassuming man, and the shortest in the class, other than me. His movements were so graceful and smooth that it looked like he was gliding on air, tossing around guys twice his size like they were rag dolls. He had a very hearty laugh that got louder and louder as he tossed my classmates and I all over the mat during each class.

At the time I was never able to use my training when I got in fights at school, which happened almost every day. The teachers never noticed my classmates picking on me, they only saw me fighting back, so I was always getting sent to the principal's office. Then I would get detention, and eventually the school notified my mother. When I told her I was just defending myself, my mother said to ignore the other students and to tell the teacher when things got out of hand. Unfortunately, it didn't work, and I kept getting in trouble. Finally, my mother threatened to take away my aikido classes if I did not stay out of trouble. Sure enough, the following week I got into a fight. I was sent to the principal's office, and my mother was called. True to her word, my mother told me that this week would be my last aikido class. I was really upset, but there was nothing I could do. I went to my sensei and explained my situation to him. He was concerned, and told my mother that if she let me continue with my aikido lessons, he promised her that I would never get into another fight at school. My mother decided to give it a chance (although I thought he was crazy). He told me to stay after class so he could show me a special technique.

After class, he asked me how the fights usually started. I told him that someone would usually push, trip, or sucker punch me. He gave me a big smile and said, 'It's very simple. Now attack me the same way.' I tried to attack him, but he grabbed my wrist with a rotating wristlock, throwing me off balance. He held onto my wrist and said, 'Try to hit me again!' The harder I tried to punch him, the harder he would crank on my wrist, which kept him from getting hit.

When I stopped trying, he smiled at me and said, 'That's what you do when someone tries to hit you. The difference is that they have not trained, so their wrists will not be as flexible as yours, and their reactions will be much different.' He made me promise to only use this move when I needed to defend myself. He said, 'Trust me and you will not get into trouble again.'

The very next day, a kid tried to pick a fight with me in class. The bully made the usual racial taunts, but before he could throw a punch, I grabbed his hand, using the technique. And it worked! He couldn't hit me when I was holding his wrist, and eventually he stopped trying. I could barely hide my satisfaction.

I now had a defensive tool to nullify attacks without having to resort to punching or kicking. Now, I didn't have to get into fights, and eventually, kids stopped picking on me because they knew I could defend myself."

* * * * *

John, Mike, and I used martial arts as the solution to handling bullies. Hopefully, by working with your child on the self-defense moves in this book, your child will also develop the mental and physical skills needed to handle his future bullies, while at the same time growing up with more confidence and higher self-esteem.

HELPING YOUR CHILD GAIN CONFIDENCE

One of the greatest gifts a parent can give their child is the gift of confidence. Actually, it can't be given or bought, but only gained, after reinforcing acts that promote confidence over and over. A parent might be able to convince their child to think and act confidently through encouragement and praise, but in reality, this kind of confidence is shallow at best. Real, lasting confidence and self-esteem can only be gained over time.

There is one basic preemptive self-defense technique that I have taught all young children, martial artist or non–martial artist: learn to project strength and confidence through assertive body language. I wanted each child to be able to address a class, an adult, or another child in a confident manner, and I had tremendous success achieving this with role-playing. I started by emphasizing that each child should relax and show a bright smile, immediately setting a positive tone. Next, I would work on getting the student to speak clearly and loudly. The last, and hardest, thing for them to do is to stop fidgeting, moving their feet back and forth, and bringing their fingers up to their mouths.

I start off getting each child accustomed to saying one or two words in class. I have them tell the class what their favorite food or color is. They didn't know that they were working on developing communicative skills, and before too long, I'd have each one of them up in front of class telling stories about their favorite subject at school. After every student spoke, I would add positive encouragement statements like, "Very good. Can you speak just a little louder?" The student would speak louder and then I would respond with, "That was wonderful!" In a short time, each student felt confident expressing themselves in front of others. Parents were always so proud and amazed when they saw their children speaking confidently in front of a group. Projecting confidence is a major factor in not being targeted by a bully.

9

Verbal Strategies for Dealing with a Bully

What can your child say to someone whose intent is to harass or demean them? There are many verbal strategies children can use to defend themselves against bullies and stop further harassment. Every situation is unique, so practice different scenarios with your child. Make sure that the intent is to elicit a laugh, defuse the situation, or just to have the bully leave, but not to make them angry.

Role-play with your child, trying to imagine different bullying scenarios he may encounter. Every situation is different, and of course, none will exactly follow any of the scripts below. The objective is to give your child some type of strategy to use when faced with these difficult situations, instead of just standing there with nothing to say.

Here are some creative comebacks I have taught my students to use in difficult situations. These types of comebacks can sometimes defuse the situation, or stop the harassment. Keep in mind that body language and vocal inflection have to be taken into consideration. A child can say the same comeback two different ways, and have two very different effects, due to the way he delivers the words. The key is not to anger the bully, but stand up to him in a creative way.

SCENARIO 1—MOCKERY

In this scenario, Amanda, a popular girl in middle school, flanked by a few of her cohorts, walks by Tina at her locker. Amanda and Tina were friends in elementary school, but no longer hang out together. Tina has been excluded from Amanda's circle of friends.

Tina: *Hey Amanda.*
Amanda: *Nice dress, Tina. Did your mommy buy it for you from the Salvation Army?*

Amanda's friends laugh.

Using some of the responses below, Tina can attempt to appeal to Amanda's conscience. Choose any of the following comebacks or make up some of your own.

- *That's pretty low, Amanda.*
- *Why do you say stuff like that?*
- *I should feel bad, but you're not worth it.*
- *You've changed, Amanda.*
- *Ouch, that hurt. Do you feel better now?*
- *Does it makes you happy to hurt my feelings?*
- *That's not funny.*
- *We used to be friends. I never thought you would act like this.*

Hopefully, these remarks will shake some sense into Amanda and her friends. There's a chance that Amanda is not aware of just how hurtful these remarks are, and only is trying to be clever in front of her friends. Most people don't want to be thought of as a bully, and if Tina can use one of these comebacks to make Amanda feel she's acting that way, she might alter her behavior.

SCENARIO 2—SPREADING RUMORS

The following situation is one that is happening more and more, with cell phones and computer technology becoming available to younger and younger children.

Clare gets a phone call from Jamie. Jamie tells Clare that she just received an e-mail from Lisa that was also sent to several other students they all know. The e-mail says that Clare slept with Bruce. Clare knows that this is not true, and is very upset that now everyone is going to be talking about it at school. Clare runs into Lisa the next day at school.

Clare: *Lisa, we need to talk.*
Lisa: *Oh, hi, Clare. What's up?*
Clare: *I heard you're spreading rumors about me.*
Lisa: *I would never do that, Clare.*
Clare: *Didn't you e-mail Jamie about me sleeping with Bruce?*

Lisa:	*Well, yeah, but I didn't make that up. I was just e-mailing her what Nancy had e-mailed me. Sorry.*
Clare:	*That's still spreading rumors about me. It's not true and why wouldn't you have asked me first? I thought we were friends.*
Lisa:	*You're right, Clare. I'm sorry.*

With modern technology, rumors can be spread with the speed of light. Now, people can say very hurtful things without having to face their victim. Clare took the first step to stopping the rumor by confronting Lisa, though she would also need to address Nancy and, by that point, probably many others to really set things right. The initial e-mail could have been simply stating that someone thought Clare might be sleeping with Bruce. But after several e-mails, it would begin to be seen as a fact.

SCENARIO 3—LUNCHTIME BULLY

Many of my students said that they were most likely to be picked on at lunchtime, in or around the cafeteria. Here, fourteen-year-old Max is sitting at a table outside the cafeteria, eating his lunch alone. Max has recently transferred to this school and hasn't has had a chance to make new friends. Along comes one of the popular students, Tim, with a few of his buddies. Tim is in the same grade as Max and is one of the larger boys in his class.

Tim:	*Hey kid.*
Max:	*Are you talking to me?*
Tim:	*Yeah, buttface. So, you're the new kid?*
Max:	*Yeah, I just moved here from—*
Tim:	*Who cares, creep? Nobody cares where you're from.*

The other kids laugh at Max. It's a difficult situation, especially since Tim is larger and stronger. There's a good chance that Max will continue to be harassed unless he stands up for himself and lets Tim know that he won't take this abuse. Max doesn't want to anger Tim, but instead hopes to impress him with his personality. In this situation, Max's tone of voice is important, and his inflection should not be argumentative or threatening.

Max's comebacks:

- *People keep telling me that I'm going to run into guys like you for the rest of my life. Great!*
- *Sorry, you've got your days mixed up. You're supposed to cut down some other new kid on Mondays.*
- *And to think we could have been best friends.*
- *All right, I heard you.*
- *Are you satisfied now?*
- *You're the king, now leave me alone.*
- *Back off, Tarzan, I'm on your side.*

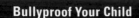
Hopefully, Max has shown his quick wit, and let Tim know that he wants to be left alone, but won't be a scapegoat for future harassment. Of course, if the situation persists or turns ugly, Max should tell a teacher or another adult.

SCENARIO 4—PLAYGROUND BULLY

The playground is another venue for the bullies to prey on their victims. In this scenario, a group of kids are kicking a soccer ball back and forth. The ball gets kicked toward Kevin, who's not part of the group. Kevin picks up the ball, but before he can throw it back, one of the kids playing, Conner, grabs the ball from him.

Conner:	*What do you think you're doing, asshole?*
Kevin:	*I was only trying to—*
Conner:	*I don't care, dude, this is our ball.*
Kevin:	*Fine, take it.*
Conner:	*You bet I will.*

In this situation, the boys are about the same size, but while Kevin doesn't want to fight, he doesn't want to be intimidated either, which could invite further bullying in the future.

Kevin's comebacks:

- *Are you done or what?*
- *Feel better now?*
- *I think you've got me confused with someone who cares.*
- *You kiss your mother with that mouth?*
- *You're wasting your breath.*
- *Oh, I see, you've got that low-self-esteem thing going on.*

Be careful, because some of these comebacks could be construed as threatening depending on the voice and attitude of the speaker. In this situation, Kevin is just standing his ground. A different tactic could be for Kevin to just to walk away, but it's likely that he will encounter Conner again, and then Connor will most likely start back up with more verbal harassment.

SCENARIO 5—PHYSICALLY THREATENING BULLY

The school bathroom is yet another place that bullies intimidate others. In this scenario, Lance is coming out of the bathroom and is forced back in by a small group of older kids. Lance is no match for these kids physically.

Lance:	*Hey, what's going on?*
Jim:	*Where do you think you're going, punk?*

Lance:	*I've got to get back to class.*
Jim:	*Not before you pay us.*
Lance:	*Pay? Pay for what?*
Jim:	*Don't be an idiot. Empty your pocket, kid.*
Lance:	*I don't have any money.*
Jim:	*Well, if you don't have money tomorrow, your ass is mine.*

Lance is in over his head here, and while there may be a chance that humor could dissuade these kids from their harassment, it's pretty unlikely. Since this situation could easily escalate, and there's no way that Lance can defend himself against all of the bigger kids, he needs to appease Jim in any manner possible, and then let a teacher know what is going on. If the teacher doesn't respond immediately, then Lance needs to inform his parents, who should talk to the principal right away. Most kids don't want to be seen as a bully, but there are predators out there that don't care one way or the other. Jim fits this bill, so Lance needs to be careful.

Lance's Comebacks:

- *I gave at the office.*
- *OK, I heard you, now let me go.*
- *This is wrong and you know it.*
- *And this seems OK to you?*

In this situation, Lance could try a bit of humor, but most likely if Jim has a history of bullying, whether he is amused or not he will still expect Lance's money the next day. At this point, an authority figure needs to intervene, to stop Jim's behavior once and for all.

10
Standing
Up to the Bully

FIGHTING VERSUS SELF-DEFENSE

Many years ago, I was a guest on *The Oprah Winfrey Show*. I was introduced as "a martial artist who believes that children should fight." As I told Oprah's audience, that is not an accurate assessment of my philosophy. As a father and a martial arts instructor, I teach children never to start a fight, but to be able to defend themselves should a fight become inevitable. I believe that there are times when a child must stand up to a bully, and children should know how to defend themselves if such a situation arises.

Here is an anecdote to illustrate my point. Recently, a diver in Australia was attacked by a great white shark while skin diving. The shark had the diver's head inside its massive jaws, when, out of desperation, the victim began to attack the shark's eyes, and finally it let him go. Incredibly, the diver survived this attack and lived to tell about it. While this is obviously a very extreme case, it is an example of knowing how to defend oneself when there is no other choice. This man didn't start a fight with the shark, but acted violently only out of self-defense.

While I was on *The Oprah Winfrey Show*, a middle school principal disagreed with my method of teaching martial arts to young children as a response to bullying. I asked him what he recommended to his own students who are being bullied, and he said that he tells them to start screaming and crying, act crazy, or run away. While that would allow the child to avoid the problem for a short period of time, the bully will still be there when the child returns the next day. Children can't scream and cry their way out of all their problems in life. Standing up to a bully can be dangerous, especially if there is a size or strength difference. But the alternative—standing there and taken a beating—is not a viable solution.

There are countless potential bullying scenarios, and each one will require a different course of action. However, there are basic do's and don'ts that your child can learn, which will help him or her know what to do when they are forced to stand up to a bully. This chapter will present some typical encounters, along with tips for how to handle them.

AWARENESS AND AVOIDANCE

Think of dealing with known or potential bullies as being like riding a bike. When you ride your bike down a street, you notice potholes in the road, garbage on the sidewalk, and people crossing the street, and you steer your bike around them. The same strategy can be applied to bullies. The Awareness and Avoidance strategy is the simplest and most basic: be aware of your surroundings and do your best to avoid the bully. Think about places where you normally find a bully, and try to stay away from them. Take a different route home, don't linger in the hallways at school, leave the park when it gets dark, etc. Simply avoid bullies as much as possible.

WALK AWAY

This is another evasive strategy to use whenever possible, especially in cases of verbal bullying: simply walk away. Regardless of the bully's taunts and the embarrassment of the situation, engaging in violence with this bully is absolutely unnecessary. No matter how hurtful the bully's words may be, try to ignore them and just walk away. If the verbal bullying persists, tell an adult, like a teacher, parent, or whoever is in a position of authority. This applies to seasoned martial artists as well as students who have had no training. If a child fights everyone who calls him a name, a good bit of his lifetime will be spent brawling. It can be difficult to just walk away, but it can also save your child from a lot of trouble, and could possibly be the end of the bullying.

I do teach one negative reality lesson to all my students: *Life is not fair.* The bully is not always going to be punished. Sometimes a bully will lose interest in a particular target, or will get in trouble once an authority figure has been alerted, but many times the harassment won't stop. This strategy and the previous one will likely only work for so long, which is why I teach my students to be proactive. Learn what to do, stay positive, and have a plan of action. If avoidance and walking away don't work, defensive action may be necessary.

As I said on *The Oprah Winfrey Show*, there's a difference between fighting and defending yourself. Make sure your child knows that fighting is a last resort, but that there are times when standing up to the bully may require them to take physical action.

Ask your child:

Parent: *If someone calls you a name, can you hit them?*
Child: *No.*
Parent: *Correct. OK, now if someone calls your mom a name, a real nasty name can you hit them then?*

Most likely your child will think for a few moments before giving you the right answer, *no.* Children are often protective of their families, and bullies realize that belittling one's parents is an easy way to provoke a fight. Teach your children to ignore the bully and walk away.

TAKING AN ASSERTIVE STAND

First your child tries to avoid the bully, but the bully finds him. The bully taunts and teases, and your child walks away. Finally, the bully encounters your child on the playground, and this time, he isn't going to let your child just walk away. As your child turns to leave, the bully steps in front of him and refuses to let him pass. Before considering any physical action, your child should try to take an assertive stand.

Taking an assertive stand means standing tall and firm, not fidgeting, and projecting calm and confidence. Positive body language is the first defense against an aggressive individual. Then, in the assertive stance, agree with the bully's taunting in a calm voice. For example, say "Yeah, I'm a geek, all right." Try to take some of the tension out of the situation with a smile, and make direct eye contact, which will show additional confidence. Though your child may be scared on the inside, the important thing is to project confidence. If the bully responds with further aggression, tell him loudly to "stop it" and to "leave me alone." Your child's confident tone of voice and delivery is extremely important here.

Practice the above with your child. Stand toe-to-toe with him and make sure he stands his ground. Have him make eye contact and tell you to leave him alone, in a confident, emphatic manner.

DEFENDING YOURSELF PHYSICALLY

There are times when, no matter how many evasive strategies have been tried, a physical confrontation is inevitable. This time, the bully disregards your child's attempt to stand up to him, and he moves to push, punch, or physically attack your child. Your child has only two choices: defend himself or get beaten up. For strategies on physical self-defense, see chapters 11 and 12.

11

The Physical Confrontation

Every confrontational situation is unique, but by following these easy-to-learn techniques, your children will have a much greater chance of handling the everyday bully. Practice these techniques with your child, or get another child to practice with him. These methods need to become ingrained in your child's mind, so that if he is in a confrontational situation, he will automatically know how to handle himself.

CONFIDENT STANCES

Before you can do any kind of blocking or self-defense, you need to learn how to be in a proper stance. My two assistants in the photos accompanying this chapter are Hunter Lane and David Fox.

Strong stances are essential for two main reasons. First, your child will be better balanced, and second, he will send a subconscious message that projects strength, not weakness.

It's easy for a child to push another child of equal weight over with one finger if they're standing with their knees locked. Try this and see: Have your child stand facing you with their knees locked, then place one finger on your child's chest and push gently. You'll find that you can move them with very little effort. Tell them to resist if they can, but they will soon realize that it's quite difficult to do.

However, once the body's center of gravity is lowered and the knees are bent to maintain a strong position, it becomes much more difficult to push someone over.

Now, have your child turn sideways so he is perpendicular to you. Have him bend his knees outward, directly over his feet, so that he slightly lowers his center of gravity. This is a much more powerful stance. Tell him to try to resist your push, then take one finger and press it against his shoulders, attempting to move him. It won't work. You will find that you'll need almost your entire body weight to move him.

Body Language

In the first series of photos, the victim is being confronted by a typical bully. Notice how weak his stance is, and the frightened look on his face.

Can you see the difference in these photos? The child has a much more powerful stance and a look of confidence on his face.

DEFENSIVE BLOCKING TECHNIQUES

I've devoted a good deal of this chapter to blocking an attack. This is the most important thing your children can learn to protect himself. Blocks are defensive moves intended to deflect blows aimed at your child. The goal isn't to learn offensive techniques, but only moves that your child can use to defend himself, that will not hurt the other child.

Defense Against a Push

Prayer Block

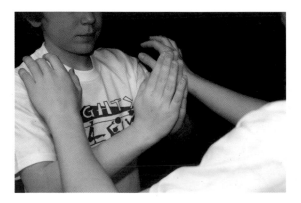

The push is the attack bullies use most often to initiate a fight. The initial shove or push is easy to defend against, using the steps below. Awareness is the key for this defensive maneuver to work. Don't allow the bully to get too close to you.

The bully steps forward and begins the pushing motion.

Have your child bring his hands together and upward, between the bully's hands.

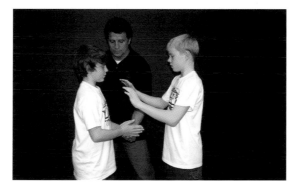

The aggressor has both of his hands almost touching the victim's shoulders, and the hands of the victim are together (as if in prayer) between the attacker's arms. Make sure your child's elbows are tucked close to his body.

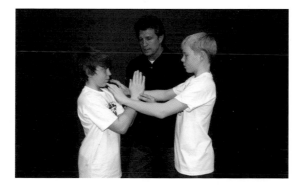

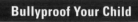

Next, before the bully's hands reach your child's shoulders, have your child rotate his arms outward, beyond his own shoulders, blocking the pushing motion by thrusting the bully's hands out to the sides. This deflecting motion takes very little effort, and will work against even a much larger bully.

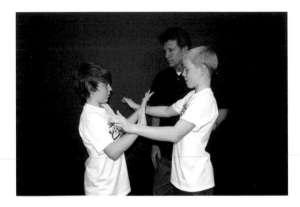

After the bully's hands are out to the sides, have your son grab the bully's wrists to secure them.

Close-up view of prayer block

The prayer block can also be used against the following attacks:

1. Two-handed grab anywhere on their body
2. Choking attempts
3. A charging attack intended to take the victim down

Defense Against a Punch or Slap

Middle block

This simple blocking maneuver enables your child to adequately block any form of swinging punch or slap directed at him. I encourage you to purchase a blocker from a martial arts product store, like The Child Blocker by Century Martial Arts Supply online (www.centuryfitness.com). The blocker is a soft striking tool that will not hurt your child's arms as you practice.

Adjust your child's stance to make it stronger, so he can utilize the block more effectively. Have him lower his center of gravity by spreading his feet wider or by shifting his back leg behind him. Also, always make sure his knees are bent aimed directly over his feet and not pushed inward.

Have your child form an X with his arms over his chest as in the first photo. X blocks are very useful because they double the strength of the block, as two arms are stronger than one. Next, have him apply force as he blocks outward with his arm as in the second photo.

Middle Block with Partner

The attacker steps forward, beginning the punch.

As the punch moves forward, have your child step backward with his right leg into a more balanced position. Also, as your child backs out of the way, have him form an X block with his arms directly in front of his chest.

Teach your child to keep his front elbow close to his body as he blocks outward. Notice in the photo how the child is standing in a strong stance with his front arm held in a guard position, not in his pockets or by his side. The back hand is tucked in by the chest in a ready position.

Close-up of middle block

The middle block can also be used against any of the following bullying attacks:

1. A slap aimed at the face
2. A grabbing attempt to the arm or shoulder
3. A kick toward the body
4. A push against their body

Defense Against a Kick

Low Block

One of the most obvious defenses when cornered is to kick the (male) aggressor in the groin. However, there are several problems with that. First, the bully is just as aware of this fact as your child, and will most likely be prepared for this kick. Next, many of the times your child is picked on, the aggressor will be someone they know, perhaps even a good friend or a sibling. We certainly don't want to teach a child to kick his own brother in the groin.

The low block is designed to protect against anyone attempting to kick your child in the groin or lower region by redirecting the kick to the outside of the victim's front leg. These photos show Keith teaching the low block.

Low Block with a Partner

The bully begins a kick aimed toward the victim's groin.

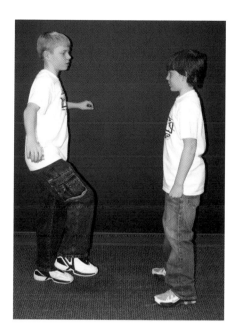

The victim steps back with his right leg as he makes an X block across his chest. By stepping backward, he gets out of range of the kick and also lowers himself into a balanced stance.

As the bully's foot rises toward his body, the victim lowers his left arm in a swinging pendulum motion, redirecting the bully's kick to the outside of his front leg.

Close-up of low block

High Block

Nothing is more vital than the protection of your child's head. With this blocking technique, your child raises his forearms over his heads to block the bully's punch. This block can also protect against some types of weapons, such as a stick. The strategy is to sacrifice an arm, if given the choice, in order to protect the head. By angling the blocking arm, it deflects the blow without absorbing its force.

Keith teaching the high block

High Block with Partner

The bully raises his arm to strike the victim on top of the head.

The victim steps back with his right leg to give himself adequate space and get into a stronger stance. He prepares by forming an X block at his chest.

As the bully follows through with his strike, the victim is in a solid stance with his front arm overhead to deflect the force of the blow.

Close-up of high block

The high block can also be used against any of the following attacks:

1. Attacks with a stick or similar type of weapon
2. Any kind of high swinging attack with hands
3. High kicks

Palm Heel Block

The palm heel block in one of the easiest blocks to learn and one of the most useful maneuvers to keep others' hand off your child. All you are teaching here is for your child to deflect blows, punches, grabs, etc., before they reach their destination. Teach the palm heel position by opening your child's hand. Bend the thumb forward and slightly curve the hand, giving it strength. The drill is to step to the outside of the incoming push or punch and push the arm away from striking. Again, we are simply redirecting the force of the blow, which takes very little effort and just requires correct timing.

Keith teaching palm heel block

Palm Heel Block with a Partner

The bully begins moving forward with a single-hand pushing motion as the victim prepares the palm heel block.

As the bully's hand approaches, the victim steps to his left at forty-five degrees as he redirects the incoming push away from his body.

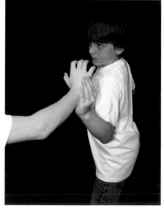

Close-up of palm heel block

In order to make this move instinctive for your child, practice by touching him lightly at different points on his body—head, shoulders, arms, etc. Have him deflect incoming touches with a very light palm heel block, until the move becomes automatic.

High X Block

The high X block is used against any attack directed toward the head.

Keith teaching high X block

High X Block with a Partner

The bully prepares to strike his victim with a punch.

As the bully steps forward, the victim steps back out of striking range and forms the X block.

The victim blocks the incoming punch by deflecting the bully's arm. This could also block any attempt to strike him with a weapon.

Close-up of high X block

Part 1—Blocking a kick

In this version of the X block, your child is learning how to block an incoming kick directed towards his middle to lower region, especially the groin area.

Keith teaching the low X block

Low X Block with Partner

The bully confronts his victim.

The bully is in the process of delivering a front kick to the victim's groin.

As the same time the kick is extending toward the victim, the victim steps backward out of range as he forms his X block.

Close-up of low X block

Part 2—Capturing the Foot

In this continuation of the low X block, we focus on capturing the bully's foot and then controlling him by turning his foot over, rendering him unable to further his attack.

The bully is in the process of extending his kick towards his victim.

The victim successfully blocks the kick.

Notice how he opens his hands, preparing to grab the foot.

The victim takes a firm hold of the attacker's foot.

Close up of him taking a firm grasp of the attacker's foot

He begins to turn the foot over, throwing the bully off balance.

Observe how he begins to rotate the bully's foot from a solid, strong stance.

He now has successfully rotated the bully so he's facing backward, off balance, and neutralized.

SELF—DEFENSE TECHNIQUES

Defense Against a One-Handed Wrist Grab

This section will teach your child how to escape from a one-handed wrist grab. Without knowing the proper technique, this hold can be difficult to escape, but it's actually quite simple to slip out of when you know how.

Here are a couple of ways to escape from the one-handed wrist grab.

Option 1: The Escape

Observe how the attacker's finger and thumb create the weak spot on the encircling hold. This is the place in the hold where you can break free. Practice this technique by grabbing your child's wrist and have him follow the illustrations.

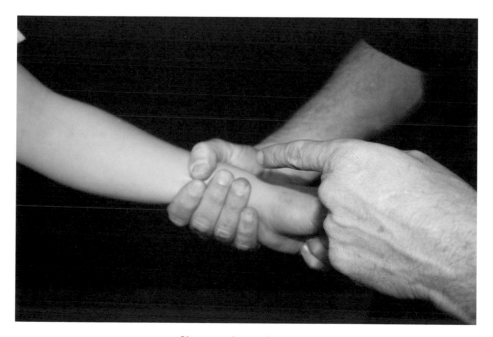

Close-up of escaping move

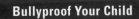

Grab the hand that's being held with your other hand to aid you as you pull away from the attacker's grasp.

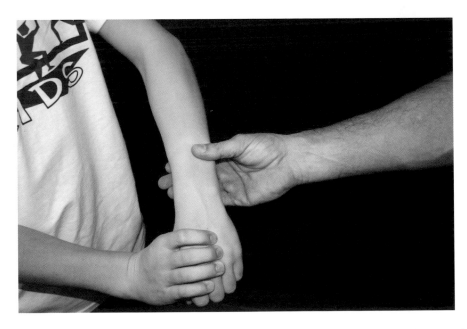

The key to escaping this hold is to twist your wrist out from the space between the attacker's finger and thumb.

Rotate your wrist out of the grasp.

Use your body in a quick twisting motion to help pull your hand out of the hold.

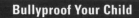

After breaking totally free, step back quickly, putting some distance between you and your attacker.

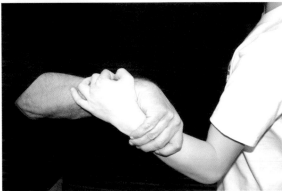

Option 2: The Capture

If you want to do more than just escape a hold, the second option is to control the bully. Using the capture, you can even bring him down to his knees, making very clear your desire to be left alone.

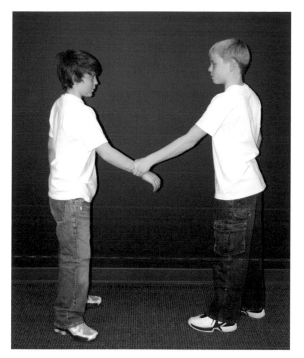

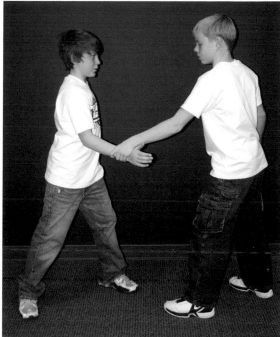

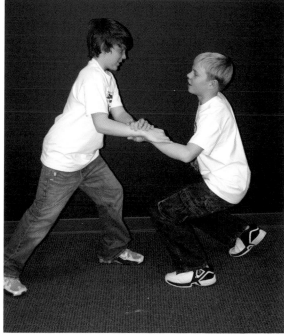

Close-up of the capture technique

Have your child open up his palm in preparation.

Next, have him firmly wrap his hand around the top of your forearm.

Have him take his free hand and place it directly over yours, locking it in place.

Your child should use his body weight to aid in the downward pushing motion with his hands. This action weakens the power of your grip and should bring you to your knees, if your child uses enough force.

Defense Against a Two-Handed Wrist Grab

Practice by grabbing your child's wrist with both hands as shown below.

As soon as you take hold of your child's wrist, have him take a firm hold of his own held hand with his other (free) hand.

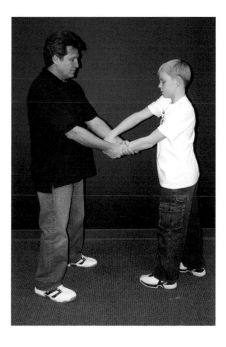

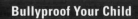
To escape this hold, have your child raise his held hand straight up toward his head, where your thumb and finger meet. The upward motion should break your hold, similar to the way it broke the hold in the one-handed grab.

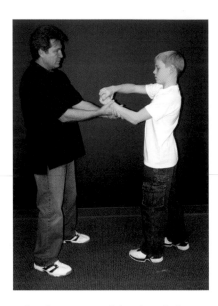

Now your child should have completely separated his hand from your hold.

Defense Against a Two-Handed Hold on the Victim's Shirt

The bad news is that this is a dangerous position for a victim who has no plan of action. From this position, the bully can do as he pleases with his victim. Also, this is an embarrassing position to be caught in in front of others. The good news is that this is one of the easiest grabs to defend against.

The victim here actually has complete control of this situation if he's properly trained. Anyone who grabs someone by their shirt, jerking them forward, doesn't understand fighting, only bullying. By grabbing their victim's shirt with both hands, the bully has basically surrendered the ability to use his hands as weapons. In other words, the bully can't use his hands to punch or push his victim if they are already holding the victim's shirt. The victim, on the other hand, still has full use of both his hands, and so has many options.

Option 1: Using Your Finger(s) as a Defensive Weapon

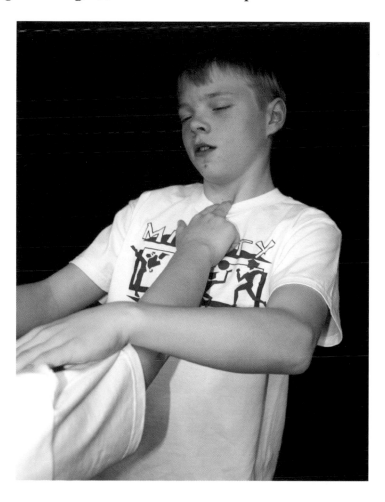

In this self-defensive scenario, work with your child by grabbing his shirt and pulling him close to you.

Have your child take one finger and raise it to your throat.

Have your child gently place one or two fingers on your throat.

Next, have him gently push (not punch or strike) against your throat, extending your arms, forcing you to release him from your hold.

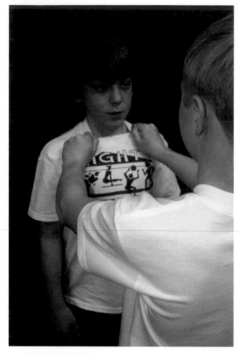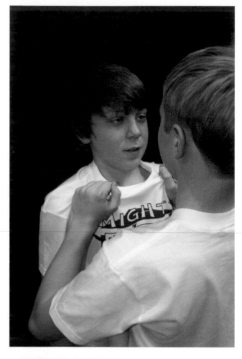

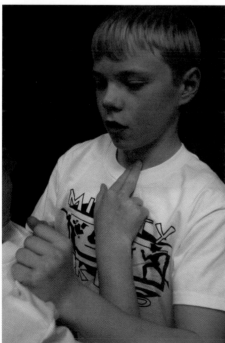

Close-ups of using the finger(s) as a weapon

Option 2: Rotating the Bully Using a Locked-arm Bar Twist

In this option, the victim must move quickly to escape, before the bully has gotten a firm hold on his shirt. When done correctly, this move will bring the bully to his knees, facing away, leaving the victim in complete control. A certain amount of force has to be used in this maneuver, but the alternative is that your child will be jerked up off his feet, left vulnerable to the bully's whim. Also keep in mind, this technique is much harder to pull off if the bully has a considerable strength or height advantage.

The bully places his hands on the victim's shirt.

Before the bully has taken a firm hold, the victim reaches over and grabs the bully's hand.

In a strong, fast motion, the victim twists the bully's wrist over, rotating his entire body.

The final move brings the bully all the way to the ground

Observe how the victim places his hand under the bully's palm, taking a firm hold of the bully's hand. If the victim moves quickly, he should able to get his hand under the bully's hand easily, but if the bully has already got a firm hold on the victim's shirt, he will need to force his hand under the bully's.

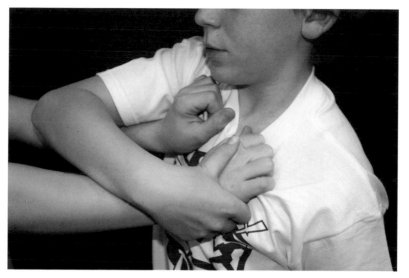

As the victim begins to rotate the bully's wrist, he gains additional leverage by placing his other hand over the bully's extended arm, forcing the bully to the ground with both hands.

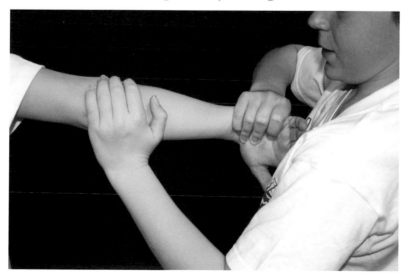

The end result is that has the bully is down on one knee, with the victim in complete control. This technique can also be used on a larger, stronger attacker. In the following set of photos, I play the role of the bully.

Notice how his hands are tucked inside of mine.

He places his other hand over my elbow.

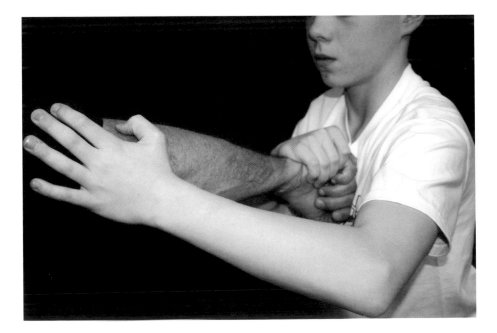

He turns and locks my arm.

He uses his body weight to force me to the ground.

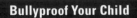
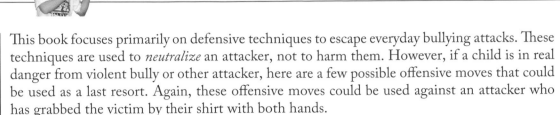

This book focuses primarily on defensive techniques to escape everyday bullying attacks. These techniques are used to *neutralize* an attacker, not to harm them. However, if a child is in real danger from violent bully or other attacker, here are a few possible offensive moves that could be used as a last resort. Again, these offensive moves could be used against an attacker who has grabbed the victim by their shirt with both hands.

Offensive moves:

- Head-butt the attacker's nose
- Open-hand slap to the attacker's face
- Backhand slap to the attacker's face
- Palm heel strike to the attacker's nose
- Back-knuckle strike to the attacker's nose
- Two-hand open-palms to the attacker's ears
- Punch to attacker's nose
- Fingers in the attacker's eyes
- Knuckles to the attacker's throat
- Finger jab to the attacker's throat
- Hammer fist to attacker's nose
- Knife-hand strike to the attacker's neck
- Reverse-knife-hand strike to the attacker's neck
- Web strike(a strike using the "web" portion of the hand, between the thumb and fingers) to attacker's throat
- Parallel elbow strike to attacker's chin
- Rising elbow strike to attacker's chin
- Twist the attacker's neck with a hair and chin grab
- Punch to attacker's solar plexus
- Elbow to attacker's solar plexus
- Knuckles to attacker's solar plexus
- Knee to attacker's thigh
- Knee to attacker's groin
- Kick to attacker's shin
- Stomp to attacker's foot

These are offensive options to choose from only if your intention is to hurt the attacker. Make sure your child understands that these are last resorts only, as they can cause severe damage.

Defense Against a Frontal Choke

There are many techniques one can use to escape a choke hold. The key to any type of effective defense is to first focus on getting the bully to release his hold around your neck, throat, or windpipe. Panic mode will set in once the ability to breathe is hindered, so a quick plan of action is imperative to accomplishing this goal.

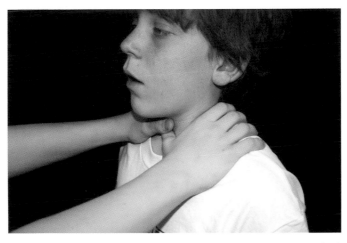

Here are three different self-defensive techniques to defend against a choke hold. Again, these measures will allow your child to control the bully, not hurt him.

Option 1: The Baseball Throw

To do the baseball throw, have your child raise his arm straight up over his head, then act as if he is throwing a baseball ninety degrees to their left. This will knock the bully's arms away, causing his grip to be released.

Practice with your child by placing your hands around your child's neck, but *do not* press in with your thumbs over his windpipe.

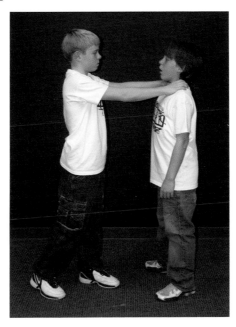

Have your child raise either one of his arms straight up, pressing his arm against his ear. This will trap your hand.

Now that your hand is trapped against your child's neck, have him rotate his body away from you.

As he rotates his body away from you, using a quick, explosive motion, he should act like he is throwing an imaginary baseball. This will knock your arms away, breaking your hold on his neck. You will be surprised how easily this technique works.

 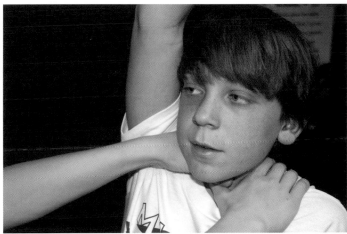

Close-ups of locking the bully's hand against their neck

Option 2: Grabbing the Thumbs, Turning them Outward

In this option, your child can release the hands wrapped around his neck by reaching in, grabbing the bully's thumbs with a firm grip, then swinging the thumbs downward and outward.

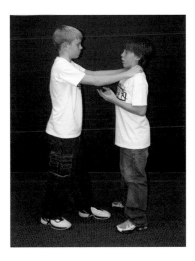

Have your child dig in if necessary to get a firm hold on your thumbs, keeping his elbows locked in close to his stomach.

Have your child step back with his back leg locked while he begins a downward pendulum swing. This will force you to bend over slightly.

Now have him gently swing your thumbs outward. Make sure he does not apply too much pressure while practicing or he could hurt your thumbs. Notice in the photo below how the victim is now in total control.

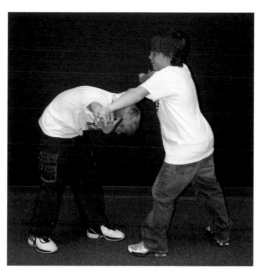

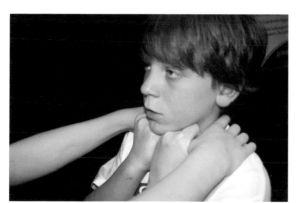

Close-up of thumb grab

Option 3: Locking Down the Thumbs

This is a more violent and painful version of the one above. Instead of bringing the bully's thumbs down and out, the victim turns the thumbs upward, pointing them to the sky. The bully's thumbs are weakest when pointed upward. Again, make sure your child keeps his elbows close to his stomach for strong support, and then, with a gentle motion, have him press your thumbs in a straight downward motion. This should buckle your knees.

Place your hands around your child's neck and have him raise his hands up between your arms once again, getting a firm hold on your thumbs.

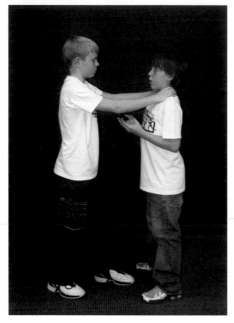 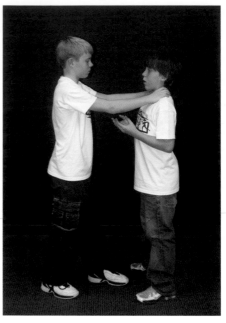

Have your child once again step back into a stronger stance while he begins turning your thumbs upward with his arms held close to his body.

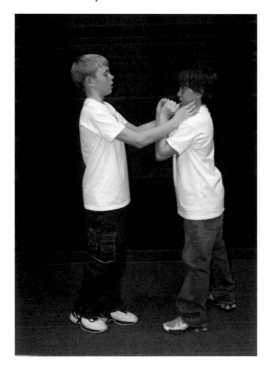

All he does now is apply gentle pressure downward, pointing your thumbs toward the ground. Where your thumbs go, you follow. Once again, the victim now controls the bully and not the other way around.

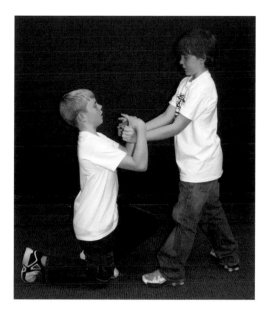

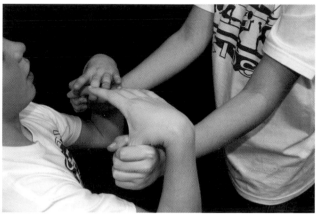

Defense Against a Headlock
Option 1: The hair grab

The headlock is one of the most common attacks that bullies used to control their victims. This seemingly playful bullying maneuver might not appear too dangerous, but it is, because the bully can potentially apply serious force to the victim's neck area.

Defending against a headlock is actually easier when your child is allowed to use full force. All it would take to defeat the bully would be a simple punch or squeezing motion to his groin. Of course, since we are teaching self-defense, not violence, it's crucial that your child learns an effective escape that will not hurting the other child.

To practice, grab your child in a sideways headlock, similar to the photo below.

Have your child spread his legs, getting into a wider stance. This will give him better balance to proceed to the next move. Then have him raise the arm closest to you straight up in the air.

Have your child take a firm hold of your hair. (Of course, have him be gentle while practicing.)

Next, have him gently pull you backward over his extended leg, which is now spread wide in a side stance.

Have him take you gently to the ground. Notice in the picture below how he continues to hold the bully's hair. In doing so, he is in total control.

Option 2: The Chin Pull

This is similar to the previous option, but can be used against a bully with no hair. Simply grab the bully under his chin and then pull him backward over your leg.

Again, grab your child in a headlock. This time, have him place his hand under your chin. Next, have your child gently pull your head back, bringing you down and over his extended leg.

 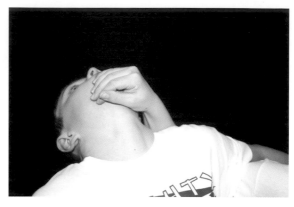

Close-ups of the chin grab

Defense Against a Rear Bear Hug

In this attack, the bully attacks his victim from behind. The key to defending against this type of attack is for your child to be aware of his surroundings at all times.

To practice, slowly sneak up behind your child.

Before you can grab your child in a tight hold from behind, have him widen his stance for better stability as he begins raising his arms from the shoulders as shown below.

As your arms surround your child, he should block you with his forearms.

Once he blocks your attack, have him step out and confront you.

Defense Against a One-Armed Attack from the Rear

In this attack, instead of bear hugging with two arms, the attacker puts one hand around the victim's neck and places the other on his arm. This is a common rear attack. It's actually more dangerous than the bear hug, because the bully has his forearm wrapped around the victim's neck. This choke hold needs to be dealt with first, before trying to get away from the attacker.

Approach your child from behind and place your hands as illustrated below.

The first move is for your child to grab your wrist and pull downward as he turns his chin to the side. As he does this, your arm is no longer pressing against his throat.

Now that your arm is no longer choking him, have him step with the leg that is closet to you, bringing it behind your body and getting into a low, balanced stance.

As your child steps behind your front leg, have him extend his front arm outward and push against your chest, forcing you backward and breaking your hold.

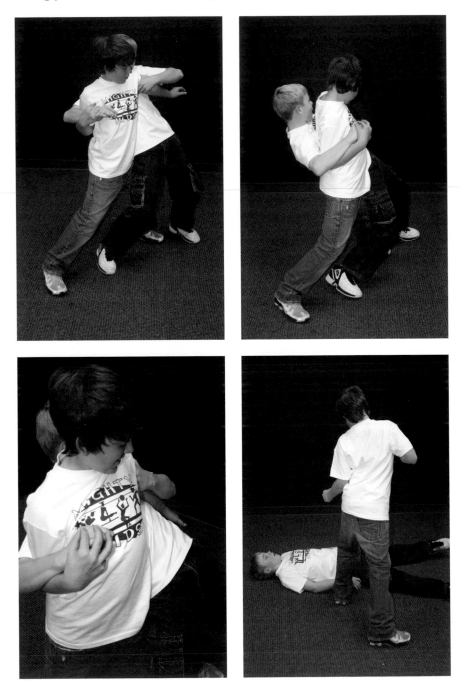

12
Ground Defenses

What should your child do to protect himself if a bully sits on top of him? In a physical confrontation, if your child can remain on his feet, he can control his movements, and is able to move away from any attack. If your child is taken to the ground, he is susceptible to punches without being able to move out of range of the incoming blows.

This chapter focuses on ground defenses. Below are easy-to-learn, effective self-defense methods for your child to use if the bully takes him to the ground. Your child is in the most perilous position on the ground, especially if the bully mounts him.

The first line of defense, if your child winds up in this position, is for your child to place his elbows as close together as possible, protecting his head with his arms. If the bully attempts to punch him in the face, he should adjust his elbows and arms to block the incoming blows. Teach your child not to panic and to remain calm. He will need to conserve his energy and focus to figure out how to escape, while the bully tires himself out.

Of course, your child should do everything possible not to wind up in this dangerous ground position where the bully has complete control of the situation. All of the alternatives should be tried first from simply avoiding the bully, walking away from his taunts, attempting to interject humor to avoid confrontation, standing up to the bully, and finally being forced to defend himself in a stand-up position.

THE ELBOWS-AND-ARMS BLOCK

ESCAPING FROM THE MOUNT POSITION

Your child needs to time this move so that it coincides with one of the bully's punches coming toward him. As the bully's punch misses or ricochets off his arm, he should quickly reach up and place one arm on the bully's neck.

At the same time that he grab the bully's neck, he should grab the bully's shoulder, arm, or shirt with his other hand, locking it into place.

Next, have your child push up with his hips, thrusting the bully upward.

As your child thrust's his hips upward, have him pull the bully's head down toward his.

Now he's is in a safer position, and is ready to make his escape.

CONTROLLING THE BULLY ON THE GROUND

Using the bully's shoulder that the victim has a firm hold of, pull him over, rolling the bully onto his back. You will need to have another child close to your child's age help to practice this maneuver over and over, until he feels comfortable rolling the other child over without too much effort.

As he rolls the bully over, he controls the bully's head while at the same time working his legs free to the side.

Notice how he lowers his head directly next to the bully's, taking away all space between them. He also lays on the bully's legs, spreading his own legs out for better leverage against the bully trying to escape. By spreading his legs and locking his arms on the bully's neck, he has successfully controlled the bully.

Caution here! Be extremely careful about having your child apply too much pressure to the bully's neck. He should not squeeze hard enough to cause pain, but just forcefully enough to hold the bully down firmly.

SOURCES AND RESOURCES

Bullystoppers.com

Coloroso, Barbara. *The Bully, the Bullied, and the Bystander: From Preschool to High School—How Parents and Teachers Can Help Break the Cycle of Violence*. New York: HarperCollins, 2004.

Craig, Wendy, and Pepler, Debra. "Bullying: Research and Interventions." *Youth Update* 15, no. 1 (1997).

Fried, SuEllen, and Fried, Paula. *Bullies and Victims: Helping Your Children Through the Schoolyard Battlefield*. New York: M. Evans, 1996.

Garbarino, James, and deLara, Ellen. *And Words Can Hurt Forever: How to Protect Adolescents from Bullying, Harassment, and Emotional Violence*. New York: Free Press, 2003.

Josephson Institute of Ethics. "The Ethics of American Youth: Violence and Substance Abuse." April 2001. http://www.josephsoninstitute.org/Survey2000/violence2000-pressrelease.htm.

North Carolina Department of Juvenile Justice and Delinquency Prevention, Center for the Prevention of School Violence

Olweus, Dan. Bullying at School: What We Know and What We Can Do. Edinburgh: Blackwell, 1993.

SafeYouth.org

Schoolbullying.com

ScienceDaily.com

WiredKids.org

Womedia.org

YouthAlternatives.com

ACKNOWLEDGMENTS

Special thanks to my wife, Kathy, who was a common-sense sounding board for this book, for her continuous love and support of my passion for children's safety issues. Special thanks also to our kids, Jennifer, Travis, and Kristen, for their love and support.

I want to thank my good friend and student, black belt Adam Brouillard, for contributing to all aspects of this book. Adam began taking martial arts from me as a child and not only advanced to the highest level, but also excelled outside of the martial arts as well. He scored a perfect SAT score of 1600 and went on to graduate from Georgia State University with honors.

Thank you David Fox, Hunter Lane, and the twins, Mathew and Michael Pigg, for assisting in the self-defense chapters.

I want to thank the following good friends and black belt experts in children's safety—Mike Genova, Frank Roberts, Keith Strandberg, John Kreng, and my brother, Rick—for their insightful contributions on bullying issues in this book.

Special thanks to my good friend, black belt Dr. Jose Luis Hinojosa, for writing the foreword to this book.

And lastly, I want to thank my own parents, whose love, support, and moral compass guided me successfully in all endeavors in life.

ABOUT THE AUTHOR

Keith Vitali began his martial arts career at the University of South Carolina in 1971 and earned his first black belt degree in tae kwon do. Keith excelled in competition, eventually winning a U.S. World Karate Championship, and was the U.S. National Karate Point Champion for three consecutive years (1978–1980). Keith's accomplishments in martial arts include being voted one of the Ten Best Fighters of All Time by *Black Belt Magazine*, being inducted into the Black Belt Hall of Fame in 1981, being named a Living Legend, and appearing on fourteen covers of national martial arts magazines.

Keith authored four successful instructional karate books: *Beginning Karate, Intermediate Karate*, and *Advanced Karate* for Contemporary Books and *Winning Tournament Karate* for Unique Publications.

Keith began his career in films as a featured player in *Force Five* and then landed a leading role in *Revenge of the Ninja* for Cannon Films, which became an international box-office hit. Next, Keith costarred with Jackie Chan in *Wheels on Meals* for Golden Harvest. Keith went on to star in *No Retreat, No Surrender 3, American Kickboxer 1, The Cut Off*, and *Superfights*. Keith produced *Superfights, Bloodmoon*, and *Your Money or Your Life* with Keith Strandberg.

Keith made national headlines with his video production company, K.V. Video Productions. Keith's first video, *Self Defense For Kids*, was an instant hit. Because of the success of the kid's video and his vast experiences in children's self-defense, Keith appeared on *The Oprah Winfrey Show* as a guest expert on child safety.

Currently, Keith is working with his nonprofit organization for young children, *Keith Vitali's K.I.D.S. Inc.* (Kids, Individual, Development and Safety).

BULLYING NOTES

JAN   2009